Just The

facts101
Textbook Key Facts

Textbook Outlines, Highlights, and Practice Quizzes

Introduction to Psycholinguistics

by Matthew J Traxler, 1st Edition

All "Just the Facts101" Material Written or Prepared by Cram101 Publishing

Title Page

STUDYING MADE EASY

This Cram101 notebook is designed to make studying easier and increase your comprehension of the textbook material. Instead of starting with a blank notebook and trying to write down everything discussed in class lectures, you can use this Cram101 textbook notebook and annotate your notes along with the lecture.

Our goal is to give you the best tools for success.

For a supreme understanding of the course, pair your notebook with our online tools. Should you decide you prefer Cram101.com as your study tool,

we'd like to offer you a trade...

Our Trade In program is a simple way for us to keep our promise and provide you the best studying tools, regardless of where you purchased your Cram101 textbook notebook. As long as your notebook is in *Like New Condition**, you can send it back to us and we will immediately give you a Cram101.com account free for 120 days!

Let The **Trade In** Begin!

THREE SIMPLE STEPS TO TRADE:

1. Go to www.cram101.com/tradein and fill out the packing slip information.

2. Submit and print the packing slip and mail it in with your Cram101 textbook notebook.

3. Activate your account after you receive your email confirmation.

* Books must be returned in *Like New Condition*, meaning there is no damage to the book including, but not limited to; ripped or torn pages, markings or writing on pages, or folded / creased pages. Upon receiving the book, Cram101 will inspect it and reserves the right to terminate your free Cram101.com account and return your textbook notebook at the owners expense.

Visit Cram101.com for full Practice Exams

"Just the Facts101" is a Cram101 publication and tool designed to give you all the facts from your textbooks. Visit Cram101.com for the full practice test for each of your chapters for virtually any of your textbooks.

Cram101 has built custom study tools specific to your textbook. We provide all of the factual testable information and unlike traditional study guides, we will never send you back to your textbook for more information.

YOU WILL NEVER HAVE TO HIGHLIGHT A BOOK AGAIN!

Cram101 StudyGuides

All of the information in this StudyGuide is written specifically for your textbook. We include the key terms, places, people, and concepts... the information you can expect on your next exam!

Want to take a practice test?

Throughout each chapter of this StudyGuide you will find links to cram101.com where you can select specific chapters to take a complete test on, or you can subscribe and get practice tests for up to 12 of your textbooks, along with other exclusive cram101.com tools like problem solving labs and reference libraries.

Cram101.com

Only cram101.com gives you the outlines, highlights, and PRACTICE TESTS specific to your textbook. Cram101.com is an online application where you'll discover study tools designed to make the most of your limited study time.

By purchasing this book, you get 50% off the normal subscription free!. Just enter the promotional code **'DK73DW20427'** on the Cram101.com registration screen.

www.Cram101.com

Learning System

facts101

Introduction to Psycholinguistics
Matthew J Traxler, 1st

CONTENTS

1. AN INTRODUCTION TO LANGUAGE SCIENCE 5
2. SPEECH PRODUCTION AND COMPREHENSION 14
3. WORD PROCESSING 23
4. SENTENCE PROCESSING 31
5. DISCOURSE PROCESSING 39
6. REFERENCE 46
7. NON-LITERAL LANGUAGE PROCESSING 53
8. DIALOGUE 60
9. LANGUAGE DEVELOPMENT IN INFANCY AND EARLY CHILDHOOD 66
10. READING 73
11. BILINGUAL LANGUAGE PROCESSING 79
12. SIGN LANGUAGE 85
13. APHASIA 91
14. RIGHT-HEMISPHERE LANGUAGE FUNCTION 97

CHAPTER OUTLINE: KEY TERMS, PEOPLE, PLACES, CONCEPTS

Definition

Phoneme

Animal communication

Displacement

Generativity

Proposition

Cohort model

Grammars

Sign

Sign language

Word order

Relative clause

Aphasia

Human evolution

Discourse

Babbling

Larynx

Vocal tract

Pidgin

Chapter 1. AN INTRODUCTION TO LANGUAGE SCIENCE

	Sign system
	Wug test
	Linguistics
	Speech production

Definition	A definition is a passage that explains the meaning of a term (a word, phrase or other set of symbols), or a type of thing. The term to be defined is the definiendum. A term may have many different senses or meanings.
Phoneme	In a language or dialect, a phoneme is the smallest segmental unit of sound employed to form meaningful contrasts between utterances. Thus a phoneme is a sound or a group of different sounds perceived to have the same function by speakers of the language or dialect in question. An example is the English phoneme /k/ (phonemes are placed between slashes in transcription), which occurs in words such as cat, kit, school, skill.
Animal communication	Animal communication is any behavior on the part of one animal that has an effect on the current or future behaviour of another animal. The study of animal communication -- sometimes called Zoosemiotics (defined as the study of sign communication or semiosis in animals; distinguishable from anthroposemiotics, the study of human communication) -- has played an important part in the methodology of ethology, sociobiology, and the study of animal cognition. Animal communication, and the understanding of the animal world in general, is a rapidly growing field.
Displacement	In linguistics, displacement is the capability of human language to communicate about things that are not immediately present.

In 1960, Charles F. Hockett proposed displacement as one of 13 'design-features' that distinguish human language from animal language:"

Honeybees use the waggle dance to communicate the location of a source of nectar. The degree of displacement in this example remains limited when compared to human language.

Generativity	Generativity in essence describes a self-contained system from which its user draws an independent ability to create, generate, or produce new content unique to that system without additional help or input from the system's original creators. In semiotics or epistemology, generativity refers to a form of communication that possesses compositionality and the ability to construct complex messages. The philosopher Daniel Dennett has argued that animals cannot have wants or desires in the sense that humans do because they lack a language with compositionality and generativity.
Proposition	In logic and philosophy, the term proposition refers to either (a) the 'content' or 'meaning' of a meaningful declarative sentence or (b) the pattern of symbols, marks, or sounds that make up a meaningful declarative sentence. The meaning of a proposition includes having the quality or property of being either true or false, and as such propositions are claimed to be truthbearers.

The existence of propositions in sense (a) above, as well as the existence of 'meanings', is disputed by some philosophers. |
Cohort model	The cohort model in psycholinguistics and neurolinguistics is a model of lexical retrieval first proposed by William Marslen-Wilson in the late 1980s. It attempts to describe how visual or auditory input (i.e., hearing or reading a word) is mapped onto a word in a hearer's lexicon. According to the model, when a person hears speech segments real-time, each speech segment 'activates' every word in the lexicon that begins with that segment, and as more segments are added, more words are ruled out, until only one word is left that still matches the input.
Grammars	Grammars: A Journal of Mathematical Research on Formal and Natural Languages is an academic journal devoted to the mathematical linguistics of formal and natural languages, published by Springer-Verlag.
Sign	A sign is something that implies a connection between itself and its object. A natural sign bears a causal relation to its object--for instance, thunder is a sign of storm. A conventional sign signifies by agreement, as a full stop signifies the end of a sentence.

Chapter 1. AN INTRODUCTION TO LANGUAGE SCIENCE

Sign language	A sign language is a language which, instead of acoustically conveyed sound patterns, uses visually transmitted sign patterns (manual communication, body language) to convey meaning-- simultaneously combining hand shapes, orientation and movement of the hands, arms or body, and facial expressions to fluidly express a speaker's thoughts. Wherever communities of deaf people exist, sign languages develop. Their complex spatial grammars are markedly different from the grammars of spoken languages.
Word order	In linguistics, word order typology refers to the study of the order of the syntactic constituents of a language, and how different languages can employ different orders. Correlations between orders found in different syntactic subdomains are also of interest. The primary word orders that are of interest are the constituent order of a clause--the relative order of subject, object, and verb; the order of modifiers (adjectives, numerals, demonstratives, possessives, and adjuncts) in a noun phrase; and the order of adverbials.
Relative clause	A relative clause is a subordinate clause that modifies a noun phrase, most commonly a noun. For example, the phrase 'the man who wasn't there' contains the noun man, which is modified by the relative clause who wasn't there. A relative clause can also modify a pronoun, as in 'he to whom I have written', or a noun phrase which already contains a modifier, as in 'the black panther in the tree, which is about to pounce'.
Aphasia	Aphasia is an impairment of language ability. This class of language disorder ranges from having difficulty remembering words to being completely unable to speak, read, or write. Aphasia disorders usually develop quickly as a result of head injury or stroke, but can develop slowly from a brain tumor, infection, or dementia, or can be a learning disability such as dysnomia.
Human evolution	Human evolution refers to the evolutionary history of the genus Homo, including the emergence of Homo sapiens as a distinct species and as a unique category of hominids ('great apes') and mammals. The study of human evolution uses many scientific disciplines, including physical anthropology, primatology, archaeology, linguistics and genetics. The evidence for human evolution is overwhelming.
Discourse	Discourse generally refers to 'written or spoken communication'. The following are three more specific definitions:•In semantics and discourse analysis: A generalization of the concept of conversation to all modalities and contexts.•'The totality of codified linguistic usages attached to a given type of social practice.

Babbling	Babbling is a stage in child development and a state in language acquisition, during which an infant appears to be experimenting with uttering sounds of language, but not yet producing any recognizable words. (Crucially, the larynx or voicebox, originally high in the throat to let the baby breathe while swallowing, descends during the first year of life, allowing a pharynx to develop and all the sounds of human speech to be formed). Babbling begins at approximately 5 to 7 months of age, when a baby's noises begin to sound like phonemes.
Larynx	The larynx, commonly called the voice box, is an organ in the neck of amphibians, reptiles (incl. birds) and mammals (including humans) involved in breathing, sound production, and protecting the trachea against food aspiration. It manipulates pitch and volume.
Vocal tract	The vocal tract is the cavity in human beings and in animals where sound that is produced at the sound source (larynx in mammals; syrinx in birds) is filtered. In birds it consists of the trachea, the syrinx, the oral cavity, the upper part of the esophagus, and the beak. In mammals it consists of the laryngeal cavity, the pharynx, the oral cavity, and the nasal cavity.
Pidgin	A pidgin language, is a simplified language that develops as a means of communication between two or more groups that do not have a language in common. It is most commonly employed in situations such as trade, or where both groups speak languages different from the language of the country in which they reside (but where there is no common language between the groups). Fundamentally, a pidgin is a simplified means of linguistic communication, as it is constructed impromptu, or by convention, between individuals or groups of people.
Sign system	A sign system is a key concept in semiotics and is used to refer to any system of signs and relations between signs. The term language is frequently used as a synonym for a sign-system. However, the term sign-system is preferable to the term language for a number of reasons.
Wug test	The wug test is an experiment in linguistics, created by Jean Berko Gleason in 1958. It was designed as a way to investigate the acquisition of the plural and other inflectional morphemes in English-speaking children. There are three plural allomorphs in English:•/z/, the most general form •/s/, which appears after voiceless consonants (cats, kæts)•/?z/, which appears after sibilants . The child is presented with a drawing of an unfamiliar creature, often blue and bird-like, and told, 'This is a wug.' (Such reasonable but nonsensical words are sometimes called pseudowords). Another wug is revealed, and the researcher says, 'Now there are two of them.
Linguistics	Linguistics is the scientific study of human language.

Chapter 1. AN INTRODUCTION TO LANGUAGE SCIENCE

	Linguistics can be broadly broken into three categories or subfields of study: language form, language meaning, and language in context.
	The first is the study of language structure, or grammar.
Speech production	Speech production is the process by which spoken words are selected to be produced, have their phonetics formulated and then finally are articulated by the motor system in the vocal apparatus. Speech production can be spontaneous such as when a person creates the words of a conversation, reaction such as when they name a picture or read aloud a written word, or a vocal imitation such as in speech repetition.
	Speech production is not the same as language production since language can also be produced manually by signs.

1. A _____ is a key concept in semiotics and is used to refer to any system of signs and relations between signs. The term language is frequently used as a synonym for a sign-system. However, the term sign-system is preferable to the term language for a number of reasons.

   a. Symbol theory
   b. Syntax
   c. Sign system
   d. Transcendent principle

2. In linguistics, _____ typology refers to the study of the order of the syntactic constituents of a language, and how different languages can employ different orders. Correlations between orders found in different syntactic subdomains are also of interest. The primary _____s that are of interest are the constituent order of a clause--the relative order of subject, object, and verb; the order of modifiers (adjectives, numerals, demonstratives, possessives, and adjuncts) in a noun phrase; and the order of adverbials.

   a. Zero-marking language
   b. Speech repetition
   c. Word order
   d. Transitional bilingualism

3. . _____ generally refers to 'written or spoken communication'. The following are three more specific definitions:•In semantics and _____ analysis: A generalization of the concept of conversation to all modalities and contexts.•'The totality of codified linguistic usages attached to a given type of social practice.

Chapter 1. AN INTRODUCTION TO LANGUAGE SCIENCE

(E.g.: legal _____, medical _____, religious _____).' •In the work of Michel Foucault, and social theorists inspired by him: 'an entity of sequences of signs in that they are enouncements (enoncés).' An enouncement (l'énoncé - often translated as 'statement') is not a unity of signs, but an abstract matter that enables signs to assign specific repeatable relations to objects, subjects and other enouncements.

a. Discourse
b. Dramatism
c. Dysphemism
d. The Establishment

4. The _____ in psycholinguistics and neurolinguistics is a model of lexical retrieval first proposed by William Marslen-Wilson in the late 1980s. It attempts to describe how visual or auditory input (i.e., hearing or reading a word) is mapped onto a word in a hearer's lexicon. According to the model, when a person hears speech segments real-time, each speech segment 'activates' every word in the lexicon that begins with that segment, and as more segments are added, more words are ruled out, until only one word is left that still matches the input.

a. Collaborative model
b. Cohort model
c. Conversational model
d. Crosslinguistic influence

5. A _____ is a passage that explains the meaning of a term (a word, phrase or other set of symbols), or a type of thing. The term to be defined is the definiendum. A term may have many different senses or meanings.

a. Demonym
b. Descriptive interpretation
c. Descriptive knowledge
d. Definition

1. c
2. c
3. a
4. b
5. d

You can take the complete Chapter Practice Test

for Chapter 1. AN INTRODUCTION TO LANGUAGE SCIENCE
on all key terms, persons, places, and concepts.

Online 99 Cents

http://www.epub4140.6.20427.1.cram101.com/

Use www.Cram101.com for all your study needs

including Cram101's online interactive problem solving labs in

chemistry, statistics, mathematics, and more.

Chapter 2. SPEECH PRODUCTION AND COMPREHENSION

CHAPTER OUTLINE: KEY TERMS, PEOPLE, PLACES, CONCEPTS

_____ | Foreign accent syndrome

_____ | Definition

_____ | Speech production

_____ | Cohort model

_____ | Homophone

_____ | Syllabification

_____ | Translation

_____ | Phonological word

_____ | Error analysis

_____ | Spreading activation

_____ | Dialogue

_____ | Formant

_____ | Speech error

_____ | Vocal tract

_____ | Coarticulation

_____ | Phoneme

_____ | Pattern playback

_____ | Speech perception

_____ | Syllable

	Duplex perception
	Allophone
	Tadoma
	Linguistics

CHAPTER HIGHLIGHTS & NOTES: KEY TERMS, PEOPLE, PLACES, CONCEPTS

| Foreign accent syndrome | Irregular repetitive speech syndrome is a rare medical condition involving speech repetition that usually occurs as a side effect of severe brain injury, such as a stroke or head trauma. Those suffering from the condition pronounce their native language with an accent that to listeners may be mistaken as foreign or dialectical. Two cases have been reported of individuals with the condition as a development problem and one associated with severe migraine. Between 1941 and 2009 there have been sixty recorded cases.

Its symptoms result from distorted articulatory planning and coordination processes. It must be emphasized that the speaker does not suddenly gain a foreign language (vocabulary, syntax, grammar, etc).. Despite a recent unconfirmed news report that a Croatian speaker has gained the ability to speak fluent German after emergence from a coma, there has been no verified case where a patient's foreign language skills have improved after a brain injury. There have been a few reported cases of children and siblings picking up the new accent from someone with foreign accent syndrome. |
| Definition | A definition is a passage that explains the meaning of a term (a word, phrase or other set of symbols), or a type of thing. The term to be defined is the definiendum. A term may have many different senses or meanings. |
| Speech production | Speech production is the process by which spoken words are selected to be produced, have their phonetics formulated and then finally are articulated by the motor system in the vocal apparatus. Speech production can be spontaneous such as when a person creates the words of a conversation, reaction such as when they name a picture or read aloud a written word, or a vocal imitation such as in speech repetition. |

Chapter 2. SPEECH PRODUCTION AND COMPREHENSION

Cohort model	The cohort model in psycholinguistics and neurolinguistics is a model of lexical retrieval first proposed by William Marslen-Wilson in the late 1980s. It attempts to describe how visual or auditory input (i.e., hearing or reading a word) is mapped onto a word in a hearer's lexicon. According to the model, when a person hears speech segments real-time, each speech segment 'activates' every word in the lexicon that begins with that segment, and as more segments are added, more words are ruled out, until only one word is left that still matches the input.
Homophone	A homophone is a word that is the same as another word but differs in meaning. The words may be spelled the same, such as rose (flower) and rose (past tense of 'rise'), or differently, such as carat, caret, and carrot, or to, two, and too. Homophones that are spelled the same are also both homographs and homonyms.
Syllabification	Syllabification is the separation of a word into syllables, whether spoken or written. It is also used to describe the process of something like a consonant turning into a syllable, but this is not discussed here. The written separation is usually marked by a hyphen when using English orthography (e.g., syl-la-ble) and with a period when transcribing in the IPA .
Translation	Translation is the communication of the meaning of a source-language text by means of an equivalent target-language text. Whereas interpreting undoubtedly antedates writing, translation began only after the appearance of written literature; there exist partial translations of the Sumerian Epic of Gilgamesh (ca. 2000 BCE) into Southwest Asian languages of the second millennium BCE. Translators always risk inappropriate spill-over of source-language idiom and usage into the target-language translation. On the other hand, spill-overs have imported useful source-language calques and loanwords that have enriched the target languages.
Phonological word	The phonological word, PrWd; symbolised as ω) is a constituent in the phonological hierarchy higher than the syllable and the foot but lower than intonational phrase and the phonological phrase. It is largely held (Hall, 1999) to be a prosodic domain in which phonological features within the same lexeme may spread from one morph to another or from one clitic to a clitic host or from one clitic host to a clitic.
Error analysis	In second language acquisition, error analysis studies the types and causes of language errors. Errors are classified according to:•modality (i.e., level of proficiency in speaking, writing, reading, listening)•linguistic levels •form (e.g., omission, insertion, substitution)•type (systematic errors/errors in competence vs.

occasional errors/errors in performance)•cause (e.g., interference, interlanguage)•norm vs. system

Methodology

Error analysis in SLA was established in the 1960s by Stephen Pit Corder and colleagues. Error analysis was an alternative to contrastive analysis, an approach influenced by behaviorism through which applied linguists sought to use the formal distinctions between the learners' first and second languages to predict errors.

Spreading activation	Spreading activation is a method for searching associative networks, neural networks, or semantic networks. The search process is initiated by labeling a set of source nodes (e.g. concepts in a semantic network) with weights or 'activation' and then iteratively propagating or 'spreading' that activation out to other nodes linked to the source nodes. Most often these 'weights' are real values that decay as activation propagates through the network.
Dialogue	Dialogue is a literary and theatrical form consisting of a written or spoken conversational exchange between two or more people. Its chief historical origins as narrative, philosophical or didactic device are to be found in classical Greek and Indian literature, in particular in the ancient art of rhetoric. Having lost touch almost entirely in the 19th century with its underpinnings in rhetoric, the notion of dialogue emerged transformed in the work of cultural critics such as Mikhail Bakhtin and Paulo Freire, theologians such as Martin Buber, as an existential palliative to counter atomization and social alienation in mass industrial society.
Formant	Formants are defined by Gunnar Fant as 'the spectral peaks of the sound spectrum P(f)' of the voice. In speech science and phonetics, formant is also used to mean an acoustic resonance of the human vocal tract. It is often measured as an amplitude peak in the frequency spectrum of the sound, using a spectrogram (in the figure) or a spectrum analyzer, though in vowels spoken with a high fundamental frequency, as in a female or child voice, the frequency of the resonance may lie between the widely-spread harmonics and hence no peak is visible.
Speech error	Speech errors, commonly referred to as slips of the tongue, are conscious or unconscious deviations from the apparently intended form of an utterance. They can be subdivided into spontaneously and inadvertently produced speech errors and intentionally produced word-plays or puns. Another distinction can be drawn between production and comprehension errors.
Vocal tract	The vocal tract is the cavity in human beings and in animals where sound that is produced at the sound source (larynx in mammals; syrinx in birds) is filtered.

	In birds it consists of the trachea, the syrinx, the oral cavity, the upper part of the esophagus, and the beak. In mammals it consists of the laryngeal cavity, the pharynx, the oral cavity, and the nasal cavity.
Coarticulation	Coarticulation in its general sense refers to a situation in which a conceptually isolated speech sound is influenced by, and becomes more like, a preceding or following speech sound. There are two types of coarticulation: anticipatory coarticulation, when a feature or characteristic of a speech sound is anticipated (assumed) during the production of a preceding speech sound; and carryover or perseverative coarticulation, when the effects of a sound are seen during the production of sound(s) that follow. Many models have been developed to account for coarticulation.
Phoneme	In a language or dialect, a phoneme is the smallest segmental unit of sound employed to form meaningful contrasts between utterances. Thus a phoneme is a sound or a group of different sounds perceived to have the same function by speakers of the language or dialect in question. An example is the English phoneme /k/ (phonemes are placed between slashes in transcription), which occurs in words such as cat, kit, school, skill.
Pattern playback	The Pattern playback is an early talking device that was built by Dr. Franklin S. Cooper and his colleagues, including John M. Borst and Caryl Haskins, at Haskins Laboratories in the late 1940s and completed in 1950. There were several different versions of this hardware device. Only one currently survives. The machine converts pictures of the acoustic patterns of speech in the form of a spectrogram back into sound.
Speech perception	Speech perception is the process by which the sounds of language are heard, interpreted and understood. The study of speech perception is closely linked to the fields of phonetics and phonology in linguistics and cognitive psychology and perception in psychology. Research in speech perception seeks to understand how human listeners recognize speech sounds and use this information to understand spoken language.
Syllable	A syllable is a unit of organization for a sequence of speech sounds. For example, the word water is composed of two syllables: wa and ter. A syllable is typically made up of a syllable nucleus (most often a vowel) with optional initial and final margins (typically, consonants).
Duplex perception	Duplex perception refers to the linguistic phenomenon whereby 'part of the acoustic signal is used for both a speech and a nonspeech percept.' A listener is presented with two simultaneous, dichotic stimuli. One ear receives an isolated third-formant transition that sounds like a nonspeech chirp.

Chapter 2. SPEECH PRODUCTION AND COMPREHENSION

CHAPTER HIGHLIGHTS & NOTES: KEY TERMS, PEOPLE, PLACES, CONCEPTS

Allophone	In phonology, an allophone is one of a set of multiple possible spoken sounds (or phones) used to pronounce a single phoneme. For example, [p?] (as in pin) and [p] (as in spin) are allophones for the phoneme /p/ in the English language. Although a phoneme's allophones are all alternative pronunciations for a phoneme, the specific allophone selected in a given situation is often predictable.
Tadoma	Tadoma is a method of communication used by deafblind individuals, in which the deafblind person places their thumb on the speaker's lips and their fingers along the jawline. The middle three fingers often fall along the speaker's cheeks with the little finger picking up the vibrations of the speaker's throat. It is sometimes referred to as 'tactile lipreading', as the deafblind person feels the movement of the lips, as well as vibrations of the vocal cords, puffing of the cheeks and the warm air produced by nasal sounds such as 'N' and 'M'.
Linguistics	Linguistics is the scientific study of human language. Linguistics can be broadly broken into three categories or subfields of study: language form, language meaning, and language in context.

The first is the study of language structure, or grammar. |

CHAPTER QUIZ: KEY TERMS, PEOPLE, PLACES, CONCEPTS

1. The _____, PrWd; symbolised as ω) is a constituent in the phonological hierarchy higher than the syllable and the foot but lower than intonational phrase and the phonological phrase. It is largely held (Hall, 1999) to be a prosodic domain in which phonological features within the same lexeme may spread from one morph to another or from one clitic to a clitic host or from one clitic host to a clitic.

    a. Praat
    b. Pre-occlusion
    c. Prodelision
    d. Phonological word

2. . _____ is the process by which spoken words are selected to be produced, have their phonetics formulated and then finally are articulated by the motor system in the vocal apparatus. _____ can be spontaneous such as when a person creates the words of a conversation, reaction such as when they name a picture or read aloud a written word, or a vocal imitation such as in speech repetition.

    _____ is not the same as language production since language can also be produced manually by signs.

    a. Speech repetition
    b. Speech shadowing
    c. Speech production

Visit Cram101.com for full Practice Exams

Chapter 2. SPEECH PRODUCTION AND COMPREHENSION

3. Irregular repetitive speech syndrome is a rare medical condition involving speech repetition that usually occurs as a side effect of severe brain injury, such as a stroke or head trauma. Those suffering from the condition pronounce their native language with an accent that to listeners may be mistaken as foreign or dialectical. Two cases have been reported of individuals with the condition as a development problem and one associated with severe migraine. Between 1941 and 2009 there have been sixty recorded cases.

   Its symptoms result from distorted articulatory planning and coordination processes. It must be emphasized that the speaker does not suddenly gain a foreign language (vocabulary, syntax, grammar, etc).. Despite a recent unconfirmed news report that a Croatian speaker has gained the ability to speak fluent German after emergence from a coma, there has been no verified case where a patient's foreign language skills have improved after a brain injury. There have been a few reported cases of children and siblings picking up the new accent from someone with _____.

   a. Spasmodic dysphonia
   b. Foreign accent syndrome
   c. Vocal fold nodule
   d. Boston Diagnostic Aphasia Examination

4. In a language or dialect, a _____ is the smallest segmental unit of sound employed to form meaningful contrasts between utterances.

   Thus a _____ is a sound or a group of different sounds perceived to have the same function by speakers of the language or dialect in question. An example is the English _____ /k/ (_____s are placed between slashes in transcription), which occurs in words such as cat, kit, school, skill.

   a. Phonetic algorithm
   b. Phonological change
   c. Phonological hierarchy
   d. Phoneme

5. A _____ is a passage that explains the meaning of a term (a word, phrase or other set of symbols), or a type of thing. The term to be defined is the definiendum. A term may have many different senses or meanings.

   a. Demonym
   b. Definition
   c. Descriptive knowledge
   d. Discourse

ANSWER KEY
Chapter 2. SPEECH PRODUCTION AND COMPREHENSION

1. d
2. c
3. b
4. d
5. b

You can take the complete Chapter Practice Test

for Chapter 2. SPEECH PRODUCTION AND COMPREHENSION
on all key terms, persons, places, and concepts.

Online 99 Cents

http://www.epub4140.6.20427.2.cram101.com/

Use www.Cram101.com for all your study needs

including Cram101's online interactive problem solving labs in

chemistry, statistics, mathematics, and more.

CHAPTER OUTLINE: KEY TERMS, PEOPLE, PLACES, CONCEPTS

Polysynthetic language

Bigram

Definition

Lexicon

Mental lexicon

Syllable

Trigram

Cohort model

Spreading activation

Latent semantic analysis

Semantic analysis

Dialogue

Symbol grounding

Logogen model

Coarticulation

Polysemy

Language processing

Phonological word

Animacy

Chapter 3. WORD PROCESSING

	Aphasia
	Sign
	Sign language

Polysynthetic language	In linguistic typology, polysynthetic languages are highly synthetic languages, i.e., languages in which words are composed of many morphemes. Whereas isolating languages have a low morpheme-to-word ratio, polysynthetic languages have extremely high morpheme-to-word ratios. Not all languages can be easily classified as being completely polysynthetic.
Bigram	A bigram is every sequence of two adjacent elements in a string of tokens, which are typically letters, syllables, or words; they are n-grams for n=2. The frequency distribution of bigrams in a string are commonly used for simple statistical analysis of text in many applications, including in computational linguistics, cryptography, speech recognition, and so on. Gappy bigrams or skipping bigrams are word pairs which allow gaps (perhaps avoiding connecting words, or allowing some simulation of dependencies, as in a dependency grammar). Head word bigrams are gappy bigrams with an explicit dependency relationship.
Definition	A definition is a passage that explains the meaning of a term (a word, phrase or other set of symbols), or a type of thing. The term to be defined is the definiendum. A term may have many different senses or meanings.
Lexicon	In linguistics, the lexicon of a language is its vocabulary, including its words and expressions. A lexicon is also a synonym of the word thesaurus. More formally, it is a language's inventory of lexemes.

Mental lexicon	The mental lexicon is a construct used in linguistics and psycholinguistics to refer to individual speakers' lexical, or word, representations. However, not all scientists agree as to the utility of the mental lexicon as a scientific construct. The mental lexicon differs from the lexicon in that it is not just a general collection of words; instead, it deals with how those words are activated, stored, processed, and retrieved by each speaker.
Syllable	A syllable is a unit of organization for a sequence of speech sounds. For example, the word water is composed of two syllables: wa and ter. A syllable is typically made up of a syllable nucleus (most often a vowel) with optional initial and final margins (typically, consonants).
Trigram	Trigrams are a special case of the N-gram, where N is 3. They are often used in natural language processing for doing statistical analysis of texts.
Cohort model	The cohort model in psycholinguistics and neurolinguistics is a model of lexical retrieval first proposed by William Marslen-Wilson in the late 1980s. It attempts to describe how visual or auditory input (i.e., hearing or reading a word) is mapped onto a word in a hearer's lexicon. According to the model, when a person hears speech segments real-time, each speech segment 'activates' every word in the lexicon that begins with that segment, and as more segments are added, more words are ruled out, until only one word is left that still matches the input.
Spreading activation	Spreading activation is a method for searching associative networks, neural networks, or semantic networks. The search process is initiated by labeling a set of source nodes (e.g. concepts in a semantic network) with weights or 'activation' and then iteratively propagating or 'spreading' that activation out to other nodes linked to the source nodes. Most often these 'weights' are real values that decay as activation propagates through the network.
Latent semantic analysis	Latent semantic analysis is a technique in natural language processing, in particular in vectorial semantics, of analyzing relationships between a set of documents and the terms they contain by producing a set of concepts related to the documents and terms. latent\ semantic\ analysis assumes that words that are close in meaning will occur close together in text. A matrix containing word counts per paragraph (rows represent unique words and columns represent each paragraph) is constructed from a large piece of text and a mathematical technique called singular value decomposition (SVD) is used to reduce the number of columns while preserving the similarity structure among rows.

Chapter 3. WORD PROCESSING

Dialogue	Dialogue is a literary and theatrical form consisting of a written or spoken conversational exchange between two or more people.
	Its chief historical origins as narrative, philosophical or didactic device are to be found in classical Greek and Indian literature, in particular in the ancient art of rhetoric.
	Having lost touch almost entirely in the 19th century with its underpinnings in rhetoric, the notion of dialogue emerged transformed in the work of cultural critics such as Mikhail Bakhtin and Paulo Freire, theologians such as Martin Buber, as an existential palliative to counter atomization and social alienation in mass industrial society.
Symbol grounding	The Symbol Grounding Problem is related to the problem of how words (symbols) get their meanings, and hence to the problem of what meaning itself really is. The problem of meaning is in turn related to the problem of consciousness, or how it is that mental states are meaningful. According to a widely held theory of cognition called 'computationalism,' cognition (i.e., thinking) is just a form of computation.
Logogen model	The logogen model of 1969 is a model of speech recognition that uses units called logogens to explain how humans comprehend spoken or written words. Logogens are a vast number of specialized recognition units, each able to recognize one specific word. This model provides for the effects of context on word recognition.
Coarticulation	Coarticulation in its general sense refers to a situation in which a conceptually isolated speech sound is influenced by, and becomes more like, a preceding or following speech sound. There are two types of coarticulation: anticipatory coarticulation, when a feature or characteristic of a speech sound is anticipated (assumed) during the production of a preceding speech sound; and carryover or perseverative coarticulation, when the effects of a sound are seen during the production of sound(s) that follow. Many models have been developed to account for coarticulation.
Polysemy	Polysemy is the capacity for a sign (e.g., a word, phrase, etc). or signs to have multiple meanings (sememes), i.e., a large semantic field.
	Charles Fillmore and Beryl Atkins' definition stipulates three elements: (i) the various senses of a polysemous word have a central origin, (ii) the links between these senses form a network, and (iii) understanding the 'inner' one contributes to understanding of the 'outer' one.
Language processing	Language processing refers to the way human beings use words to communicate ideas and feelings, and how such communications are processed and understood. Thus it is how the brain creates and understands language.

Phonological word	The phonological word, PrWd; symbolised as ω) is a constituent in the phonological hierarchy higher than the syllable and the foot but lower than intonational phrase and the phonological phrase. It is largely held (Hall, 1999) to be a prosodic domain in which phonological features within the same lexeme may spread from one morph to another or from one clitic to a clitic host or from one clitic host to a clitic.
Animacy	Animacy is a grammatical and/or semantic category of nouns based on how sentient or alive the referent of the noun in a given taxonomic scheme is. Animacy can have various effects on the grammar of a language, such as choice of pronoun (what/who), case endings, word order, or the form a verb takes when it is associated with that noun. In languages which demonstrate animacy, some have simple systems where nouns are either animate (e.g. people, animals) or inanimate (e.g. buildings, trees, abstract ideas), whereas others have complex hierarchical systems.
Aphasia	Aphasia is an impairment of language ability. This class of language disorder ranges from having difficulty remembering words to being completely unable to speak, read, or write. Aphasia disorders usually develop quickly as a result of head injury or stroke, but can develop slowly from a brain tumor, infection, or dementia, or can be a learning disability such as dysnomia.
Sign	A sign is something that implies a connection between itself and its object. A natural sign bears a causal relation to its object--for instance, thunder is a sign of storm. A conventional sign signifies by agreement, as a full stop signifies the end of a sentence.
Sign language	A sign language is a language which, instead of acoustically conveyed sound patterns, uses visually transmitted sign patterns (manual communication, body language) to convey meaning--simultaneously combining hand shapes, orientation and movement of the hands, arms or body, and facial expressions to fluidly express a speaker's thoughts. Wherever communities of deaf people exist, sign languages develop. Their complex spatial grammars are markedly different from the grammars of spoken languages.

Chapter 3. WORD PROCESSING

1. _____s are a special case of the N-gram, where N is 3. They are often used in natural language processing for doing statistical analysis of texts.

   a. Vocapia Research
   b. Trigram
   c. Voice command device
   d. Voice Finger

2. In linguistic typology, _____s are highly synthetic languages, i.e., languages in which words are composed of many morphemes. Whereas isolating languages have a low morpheme-to-word ratio, _____s have extremely high morpheme-to-word ratios.

   Not all languages can be easily classified as being completely polysynthetic.

   a. Pro-drop language
   b. Polysynthetic language
   c. Secundative language
   d. Split ergativity

3. A _____ is a passage that explains the meaning of a term (a word, phrase or other set of symbols), or a type of thing. The term to be defined is the definiendum. A term may have many different senses or meanings.

   a. Demonym
   b. Definition
   c. Descriptive knowledge
   d. Discourse

4. The _____ in psycholinguistics and neurolinguistics is a model of lexical retrieval first proposed by William Marslen-Wilson in the late 1980s. It attempts to describe how visual or auditory input (i.e., hearing or reading a word) is mapped onto a word in a hearer's lexicon. According to the model, when a person hears speech segments real-time, each speech segment 'activates' every word in the lexicon that begins with that segment, and as more segments are added, more words are ruled out, until only one word is left that still matches the input.

   a. Collaborative model
   b. Competition model
   c. Cohort model
   d. Crosslinguistic influence

5. . _____ refers to the way human beings use words to communicate ideas and feelings, and how such communications are processed and understood. Thus it is how the brain creates and understands language. Most recent theories consider that this process is carried out entirely by and inside the brain.

   a. Language production
   b. Lethologica
   c. Lexicalisation

ANSWER KEY
Chapter 3. WORD PROCESSING

---

1. b
2. b
3. b
4. c
5. d

You can take the complete Chapter Practice Test

for Chapter 3. WORD PROCESSING
on all key terms, persons, places, and concepts.

Online 99 Cents

http://www.epub4140.6.20427.3.cram101.com/

Use www.Cram101.com for all your study needs

including Cram101's online interactive problem solving labs in

chemistry, statistics, mathematics, and more.

Chapter 4. SENTENCE PROCESSING

CHAPTER OUTLINE: KEY TERMS, PEOPLE, PLACES, CONCEPTS

Definition

Syntactic ambiguity

Syntax

Cohort model

Sign

Sign language

Relative clause

Context

Reduced relative clause

Animacy

Construals

Filler

Grammars

Chapter 4. SENTENCE PROCESSING

Definition	A definition is a passage that explains the meaning of a term (a word, phrase or other set of symbols), or a type of thing. The term to be defined is the definiendum. A term may have many different senses or meanings.
Syntactic ambiguity	Syntactic ambiguity is a property of sentences which may be reasonably interpreted in more than one way, or reasonably interpreted to mean more than one thing. Ambiguity may or may not involve one word having two parts of speech or homonyms.
	Syntactic ambiguity arises not from the range of meanings of single words, but from the relationship between the words and clauses of a sentence, and the sentence structure implied thereby.
Syntax	In linguistics, syntax is the study of the principles and rules for constructing phrases and sentences in natural languages.
	In addition to referring to the overarching discipline, the term syntax is also used to refer directly to the rules and principles that govern the sentence structure of any individual language, as in 'the syntax of Modern Irish.' Modern research in syntax attempts to describe languages in terms of such rules. Many professionals in this discipline attempt to find general rules that apply to all natural languages.
Cohort model	The cohort model in psycholinguistics and neurolinguistics is a model of lexical retrieval first proposed by William Marslen-Wilson in the late 1980s. It attempts to describe how visual or auditory input (i.e., hearing or reading a word) is mapped onto a word in a hearer's lexicon. According to the model, when a person hears speech segments real-time, each speech segment 'activates' every word in the lexicon that begins with that segment, and as more segments are added, more words are ruled out, until only one word is left that still matches the input.
Sign	A sign is something that implies a connection between itself and its object. A natural sign bears a causal relation to its object--for instance, thunder is a sign of storm. A conventional sign signifies by agreement, as a full stop signifies the end of a sentence.
Sign language	A sign language is a language which, instead of acoustically conveyed sound patterns, uses visually transmitted sign patterns (manual communication, body language) to convey meaning--simultaneously combining hand shapes, orientation and movement of the hands, arms or body, and facial expressions to fluidly express a speaker's thoughts.
	Wherever communities of deaf people exist, sign languages develop. Their complex spatial grammars are markedly different from the grammars of spoken languages.

Relative clause	A relative clause is a subordinate clause that modifies a noun phrase, most commonly a noun. For example, the phrase 'the man who wasn't there' contains the noun man, which is modified by the relative clause who wasn't there. A relative clause can also modify a pronoun, as in 'he to whom I have written', or a noun phrase which already contains a modifier, as in 'the black panther in the tree, which is about to pounce'.
Context	Context is a notion used in the language sciences (linguistics, sociolinguistics, systemic functional linguistics, discourse analysis, pragmatics, semiotics, etc). in two different ways, namely as•verbal context•social context Verbal context Verbal context refers to surrounding text or talk of an expression (word, sentence, conversational turn, speech act, etc).. The idea is that verbal context influences the way we understand the expression.
Reduced relative clause	A reduced relative clause is a relative clause that is not marked by an overt complementizer (such as that). Reduced relative clauses often give rise to ambiguity or garden path effects, and have been a common topic of psycholinguistic study, especially in the field of sentence processing. Relative clauses are a special class of dependent clause (also called 'subordinate clause') that serve to modify a noun.
Animacy	Animacy is a grammatical and/or semantic category of nouns based on how sentient or alive the referent of the noun in a given taxonomic scheme is. Animacy can have various effects on the grammar of a language, such as choice of pronoun (what/who), case endings, word order, or the form a verb takes when it is associated with that noun. In languages which demonstrate animacy, some have simple systems where nouns are either animate (e.g. people, animals) or inanimate (e.g. buildings, trees, abstract ideas), whereas others have complex hierarchical systems.
Construals	Construal is a social psychological term used to describe how a person perceives, comprehends, and interprets the world around him or her, particularly the behavior or action of others towards him or her. Researchers and theorists within virtually every sub-discipline of psychology have acknowledged the relevance of a subjective construal, especially with regards to the concepts of the false consensus effect and the fundamental attribution error. It is important to note that there is a difference between self-construal and construal in a social atmosphere. While self-construal is a perception of the self, the latter is a perception of one's surroundings.

Chapter 4. SENTENCE PROCESSING

Construal plays a crucial role in situations 'whenever people are obliged to venture beyond the information immediately provided by the direct observation or secondhand report of a stimulus event, in particular whenever they are obliged to infer additional details of content, context, or meaning in the actions and outcomes that unfold around them.' In other words, a person is most likely to use construal when he or she lacks the knowledge to correctly deal with a given situation.

The concept of construal is not a new one, and the components of construal can be seen in the works of many past psychologists including Kurt Lewin's recognition of the importance of a subjective reality and its impact on one's personal significance; Kurt Koffka's theories of gestalt psychology; Brunswik's emphasis on subjective distinction; Murray's discussion of 'beta press'; Kelly's account of personal constructs; Merleau-Ponty's reference to personal situations; and more recent discussions by personality theorists such as Endler and Pervin. Construal used to be viewed as an obstruction in one's perception of the world, but has evolved into a mechanism used to explain how or why a person thinks the way they do.

Cognitive psychologists have been perhaps the most preoccupied with the idea of construal. This is evident in their emphasis on a human's formation of schemas 'that help perceivers to resolve ambiguity, fill in the gaps, and generally perceive predictability and coherence.' They focus on the idea that we rely on other sources to form our ideas of our surroundings.

Solomon Asch presented an important concept in construal theory when he stated, 'that the very meaning of a message can change as a function of the source to which it is attributed.' His most classic example is the effect of the phrase 'a little rebellion...is a good thing.' This statement coming from Thomas Jefferson has a different meaning to the recipient than it does coming from V.I. Lenin. The meaning of the statement is dependent on not only who says it, but also on how the recipient of the message interprets it.

There are three major sources of construal in human beings: the need to feel good about ourselves, the need to be accurate, and the need to belong. The American social psychologist, Leon Festinger, was one of the first to acknowledge that these needs may not always coincide . Another important psychologist with prevalence to construal is Austrian Fritz Heider, who made the concept of construal clear when he said, 'Generally, a person reacts to what he thinks the other person is perceiving, feeling, and thinking, in addition to what the other person may be doing.' In other words, a person bases his or her opinions and actions on the opinions and action of everybody else.

For example, take this situation into consideration:

Christopher likes Samantha and wants to ask her to the school prom. He is shy and concerned that Samantha may respond negatively.

A social psychologist observes not only Samantha's behavior towards Christopher, but also how Christopher perceives and interprets her behavior toward him. An objective observer may perceive Samantha smiling as friendly, but Christopher may think that she is laughing at something in his appearance, and as a result, he might not invite her.

Contemporary views on construal include the concepts of naïve realism, the accessibility principle, and a focus on the idea of self-construal. Lee Ross' concept of naïve realism is especially important in the context of construal. It is the conviction all of us have that we perceive things how they really are. Essentially, people acknowledge the fact that others experience the effects of construal, but personally think that they form their own thoughts without being affected by construal. Being blinded by this process often leads individuals to commit the fundamental attribution error. Similar to Asch's theory, the accessibility principle suggests that 'mental construals are based on the information that is most accessible at the time applies to how we make sense of new information as well as to how we form judgments based on information retrieved from memory'.

| Filler | In linguistics, a filler is a sound or word that is spoken in conversation by one participant to signal to others that he/she has paused to think but is not yet finished speaking. These are not to be confused with placeholder names, such as thingamajig, which refer to objects or people whose names are temporarily forgotten, irrelevant, or unknown. Different languages have different characteristic filler sounds; in English, the most common filler sounds are uh , er and um . |

| Grammars | Grammars: A Journal of Mathematical Research on Formal and Natural Languages is an academic journal devoted to the mathematical linguistics of formal and natural languages, published by Springer-Verlag. |

Chapter 4. SENTENCE PROCESSING

1. _____ is a grammatical and/or semantic category of nouns based on how sentient or alive the referent of the noun in a given taxonomic scheme is. _____ can have various effects on the grammar of a language, such as choice of pronoun (what/who), case endings, word order, or the form a verb takes when it is associated with that noun.

    In languages which demonstrate _____, some have simple systems where nouns are either animate (e.g. people, animals) or inanimate (e.g. buildings, trees, abstract ideas), whereas others have complex hierarchical systems.

    a. Apophony
    b. Animacy
    c. Endocentric
    d. Inflected preposition

2. A _____ is a subordinate clause that modifies a noun phrase, most commonly a noun. For example, the phrase 'the man who wasn't there' contains the noun man, which is modified by the _____ who wasn't there. A _____ can also modify a pronoun, as in 'he to whom I have written', or a noun phrase which already contains a modifier, as in 'the black panther in the tree, which is about to pounce'.

    a. Resultative
    b. Sentence arrangement
    c. Relative clause
    d. Sentence-final particle

3. In linguistics, a _____ is a sound or word that is spoken in conversation by one participant to signal to others that he/she has paused to think but is not yet finished speaking. These are not to be confused with placeholder names, such as thingamajig, which refer to objects or people whose names are temporarily forgotten, irrelevant, or unknown. Different languages have different characteristic _____ sounds; in English, the most common _____ sounds are uh , er and um .

    a. Boston Diagnostic Aphasia Examination
    b. Crocodile tears
    c. Filler
    d. Defensive attribution hypothesis

4. . In linguistics, _____ is the study of the principles and rules for constructing phrases and sentences in natural languages.

    In addition to referring to the overarching discipline, the term _____ is also used to refer directly to the rules and principles that govern the sentence structure of any individual language, as in 'the _____ of Modern Irish.' Modern research in _____ attempts to describe languages in terms of such rules. Many professionals in this discipline attempt to find general rules that apply to all natural languages.

    a. Clitic
    b. Code-mixing
    c. Colorless green ideas sleep furiously

Chapter 4. SENTENCE PROCESSING

5. A _____ is a passage that explains the meaning of a term (a word, phrase or other set of symbols), or a type of thing. The term to be defined is the definiendum. A term may have many different senses or meanings.

    a. Definition
    b. Descriptive interpretation
    c. Descriptive knowledge
    d. Discourse

1. b
2. c
3. c
4. d
5. a

You can take the complete Chapter Practice Test

for Chapter 4. SENTENCE PROCESSING
on all key terms, persons, places, and concepts.

Online 99 Cents

http://www.epub4140.6.20427.4.cram101.com/

Use www.Cram101.com for all your study needs

including Cram101's online interactive problem solving labs in

chemistry, statistics, mathematics, and more.

CHAPTER OUTLINE: KEY TERMS, PEOPLE, PLACES, CONCEPTS

Definition

Discourse

Context

Proposition

Spreading activation

Error analysis

Reference

Formant

Iconicity

Cohort model

Markedness

Chapter 5. DISCOURSE PROCESSING

Definition	A definition is a passage that explains the meaning of a term (a word, phrase or other set of symbols), or a type of thing. The term to be defined is the definiendum. A term may have many different senses or meanings.
Discourse	Discourse generally refers to 'written or spoken communication'. The following are three more specific definitions:•In semantics and discourse analysis: A generalization of the concept of conversation to all modalities and contexts.•'The totality of codified linguistic usages attached to a given type of social practice. (E.g.: legal discourse, medical discourse, religious discourse).' •In the work of Michel Foucault, and social theorists inspired by him: 'an entity of sequences of signs in that they are enouncements (enoncés).' An enouncement (l'énoncé - often translated as 'statement') is not a unity of signs, but an abstract matter that enables signs to assign specific repeatable relations to objects, subjects and other enouncements.
Context	Context is a notion used in the language sciences (linguistics, sociolinguistics, systemic functional linguistics, discourse analysis, pragmatics, semiotics, etc). in two different ways, namely as•verbal context•social context Verbal context Verbal context refers to surrounding text or talk of an expression (word, sentence, conversational turn, speech act, etc).. The idea is that verbal context influences the way we understand the expression.
Proposition	In logic and philosophy, the term proposition refers to either (a) the 'content' or 'meaning' of a meaningful declarative sentence or (b) the pattern of symbols, marks, or sounds that make up a meaningful declarative sentence. The meaning of a proposition includes having the quality or property of being either true or false, and as such propositions are claimed to be truthbearers. The existence of propositions in sense (a) above, as well as the existence of 'meanings', is disputed by some philosophers.
Spreading activation	Spreading activation is a method for searching associative networks, neural networks, or semantic networks. The search process is initiated by labeling a set of source nodes (e.g. concepts in a semantic network) with weights or 'activation' and then iteratively propagating or 'spreading' that activation out to other nodes linked to the source nodes. Most often these 'weights' are real values that decay as activation propagates through the network.
Error analysis	In second language acquisition, error analysis studies the types and causes of language errors. Errors are classified according to:•modality (i.e., level of proficiency in speaking, writing, reading, listening)•linguistic levels •form (e.g., omission, insertion, substitution)•type (systematic errors/errors in competence vs.

occasional errors/errors in performance)•cause (e.g., interference, interlanguage)•norm vs. system

Methodology

Error analysis in SLA was established in the 1960s by Stephen Pit Corder and colleagues. Error analysis was an alternative to contrastive analysis, an approach influenced by behaviorism through which applied linguists sought to use the formal distinctions between the learners' first and second languages to predict errors.

Reference	The word reference is derived from Middle English referren, from Middle French référer, from Latin referre, 'to carry back', formed from the prefix re- and ferre, 'to bear'. A large number of words derive from this root, including referee, reference, referendum, all retaining the basic meaning of the original Latin as 'a point, place or source of origin' in terms of which something of comparable nature can be defined. A referee is the provider of this source of origin, and a referent is the possessor of the source of origin, whether it is knowledge, matter or energy.
Formant	Formants are defined by Gunnar Fant as 'the spectral peaks of the sound spectrum P(f)' of the voice. In speech science and phonetics, formant is also used to mean an acoustic resonance of the human vocal tract. It is often measured as an amplitude peak in the frequency spectrum of the sound, using a spectrogram (in the figure) or a spectrum analyzer, though in vowels spoken with a high fundamental frequency, as in a female or child voice, the frequency of the resonance may lie between the widely-spread harmonics and hence no peak is visible.
Iconicity	In functional-cognitive linguistics, as well as in semiotics, iconicity is the conceived similarity or analogy between the form of a sign (linguistic or otherwise) and its meaning, as opposed to arbitrariness.

Iconic principles:•Quantity principle: conceptual complexity corresponds to formal complexity•Proximity principle: conceptual distance tends to match with linguistic distance•Sequential order principle: the sequential order of events described is mirrored in the speech chainQuantity principle

The use of quantity of phonetic material to iconically mark increased quality or quantity can be noted in the lengthening of words to indicate a greater degree, such as 'looong'. It is also common to use reduplication to iconically mark increase, as Sapir is often quoted, 'The process is generally employed, with self-evident symbolism, to indicate such concepts as distribution, plurality, repetition, customary activity, increase of size, added intensity, continuance' (1921:79). |
| Cohort model | The cohort model in psycholinguistics and neurolinguistics is a model of lexical retrieval first proposed by William Marslen-Wilson in the late 1980s. |

Chapter 5. DISCOURSE PROCESSING

	It attempts to describe how visual or auditory input (i.e., hearing or reading a word) is mapped onto a word in a hearer's lexicon. According to the model, when a person hears speech segments real-time, each speech segment 'activates' every word in the lexicon that begins with that segment, and as more segments are added, more words are ruled out, until only one word is left that still matches the input.
Markedness	Markedness is a specific kind of asymmetry relationship between elements of linguistic or conceptual structure. In a marked-unmarked relation, one term of an opposition is the broader, dominant one. The dominant term is known as the 'unmarked' term and the other, secondary one is the 'marked' term.

1. A _____ is a passage that explains the meaning of a term (a word, phrase or other set of symbols), or a type of thing. The term to be defined is the definiendum. A term may have many different senses or meanings.

   a. Definition
   b. Descriptive interpretation
   c. Descriptive knowledge
   d. Discourse

2. The _____ in psycholinguistics and neurolinguistics is a model of lexical retrieval first proposed by William Marslen-Wilson in the late 1980s. It attempts to describe how visual or auditory input (i.e., hearing or reading a word) is mapped onto a word in a hearer's lexicon. According to the model, when a person hears speech segments real-time, each speech segment 'activates' every word in the lexicon that begins with that segment, and as more segments are added, more words are ruled out, until only one word is left that still matches the input.

   a. Collaborative model
   b. Competition model
   c. Cohort model
   d. Crosslinguistic influence

3. . _____ is a notion used in the language sciences (linguistics, sociolinguistics, systemic functional linguistics, discourse analysis, pragmatics, semiotics, etc). in two different ways, namely as•verbal _____ •social _____

   Verbal _____

   Verbal _____ refers to surrounding text or talk of an expression (word, sentence, conversational turn, speech act, etc).. The idea is that verbal _____ influences the way we understand the expression.

   a. Cataphora
   b. Communicative rationality

Visit Cram101.com for full Practice Exams

c. Cooperative principle

d. Context

4. In second language acquisition, _____ studies the types and causes of language errors. Errors are classified according to:•modality (i.e., level of proficiency in speaking, writing, reading, listening)•linguistic levels •form (e.g., omission, insertion, substitution)•type (systematic errors/errors in competence vs. occasional errors/errors in performance)•cause (e.g., interference, interlanguage)•norm vs. system

Methodology

_____ in SLA was established in the 1960s by Stephen Pit Corder and colleagues. _____ was an alternative to contrastive analysis, an approach influenced by behaviorism through which applied linguists sought to use the formal distinctions between the learners' first and second languages to predict errors.

a. West Coast Conference on Formal Linguistics

b. Symbol grounding

c. Triangle of reference

d. Error analysis

5. _____ generally refers to 'written or spoken communication'. The following are three more specific definitions:•In semantics and _____ analysis: A generalization of the concept of conversation to all modalities and contexts.•'The totality of codified linguistic usages attached to a given type of social practice. (E.g.: legal _____, medical _____, religious _____).' •In the work of Michel Foucault, and social theorists inspired by him: 'an entity of sequences of signs in that they are enouncements (enoncés).' An enouncement (l'énoncé - often translated as 'statement') is not a unity of signs, but an abstract matter that enables signs to assign specific repeatable relations to objects, subjects and other enouncements.

a. Discourse

b. Dramatism

c. Dysphemism

d. The Establishment

1. a
2. c
3. d
4. d
5. a

You can take the complete Chapter Practice Test

for Chapter 5. DISCOURSE PROCESSING
on all key terms, persons, places, and concepts.

Online 99 Cents

http://www.epub4140.6.20427.5.cram101.com/

Use www.Cram101.com for all your study needs

including Cram101's online interactive problem solving labs in

chemistry, statistics, mathematics, and more.

Chapter 6. REFERENCE

	Definition
	Discourse
	Reference
	Context
	Word order
	Cohort model
	Aphasia
	Implicature
	Sign
	Sign language
	Animacy

CHAPTER HIGHLIGHTS & NOTES: KEY TERMS, PEOPLE, PLACES, CONCEPTS

Definition	A definition is a passage that explains the meaning of a term (a word, phrase or other set of symbols), or a type of thing. The term to be defined is the definiendum. A term may have many different senses or meanings.
Discourse	Discourse generally refers to 'written or spoken communication'. The following are three more specific definitions:•In semantics and discourse analysis: A generalization of the concept of conversation to all modalities and contexts.•'The totality of codified linguistic usages attached to a given type of social practice.

Chapter 6. REFERENCE

47

CHAPTER HIGHLIGHTS & NOTES: KEY TERMS, PEOPLE, PLACES, CONCEPTS

Reference	The word reference is derived from Middle English referren, from Middle French référer, from Latin referre, 'to carry back', formed from the prefix re- and ferre, 'to bear'. A large number of words derive from this root, including referee, reference, referendum, all retaining the basic meaning of the original Latin as 'a point, place or source of origin' in terms of which something of comparable nature can be defined. A referee is the provider of this source of origin, and a referent is the possessor of the source of origin, whether it is knowledge, matter or energy.
Context	Context is a notion used in the language sciences (linguistics, sociolinguistics, systemic functional linguistics, discourse analysis, pragmatics, semiotics, etc). in two different ways, namely as·verbal context·social context Verbal context Verbal context refers to surrounding text or talk of an expression (word, sentence, conversational turn, speech act, etc).. The idea is that verbal context influences the way we understand the expression.
Word order	In linguistics, word order typology refers to the study of the order of the syntactic constituents of a language, and how different languages can employ different orders. Correlations between orders found in different syntactic subdomains are also of interest. The primary word orders that are of interest are the constituent order of a clause--the relative order of subject, object, and verb; the order of modifiers (adjectives, numerals, demonstratives, possessives, and adjuncts) in a noun phrase; and the order of adverbials.
Cohort model	The cohort model in psycholinguistics and neurolinguistics is a model of lexical retrieval first proposed by William Marslen-Wilson in the late 1980s. It attempts to describe how visual or auditory input (i.e., hearing or reading a word) is mapped onto a word in a hearer's lexicon. According to the model, when a person hears speech segments real-time, each speech segment 'activates' every word in the lexicon that begins with that segment, and as more segments are added, more words are ruled out, until only one word is left that still matches the input.
Aphasia	Aphasia is an impairment of language ability. This class of language disorder ranges from having difficulty remembering words to being completely unable to speak, read, or write. Aphasia disorders usually develop quickly as a result of head injury or stroke, but can develop slowly from a brain tumor, infection, or dementia, or can be a learning disability such as dysnomia.
Implicature	Implicature is a technical term in the pragmatics subfield of linguistics, coined by H. P.

Visit Cram101.com for full Practice Exams

Chapter 6. REFERENCE

	Grice, which refers to what is suggested in an utterance, even though neither expressed nor strictly implied (that is, entailed) by the utterance. For example, the sentence 'Mary had a baby and got married' strongly suggests that Mary had the baby before the wedding, but the sentence would still be strictly true if Mary had her baby after she got married. Further, if we add the qualification '-- not necessarily in that order' to the original sentence, then the implicature is cancelled even though the meaning of the original sentence is not altered.
Sign	A sign is something that implies a connection between itself and its object. A natural sign bears a causal relation to its object--for instance, thunder is a sign of storm. A conventional sign signifies by agreement, as a full stop signifies the end of a sentence.
Sign language	A sign language is a language which, instead of acoustically conveyed sound patterns, uses visually transmitted sign patterns (manual communication, body language) to convey meaning-- simultaneously combining hand shapes, orientation and movement of the hands, arms or body, and facial expressions to fluidly express a speaker's thoughts. Wherever communities of deaf people exist, sign languages develop. Their complex spatial grammars are markedly different from the grammars of spoken languages.
Animacy	Animacy is a grammatical and/or semantic category of nouns based on how sentient or alive the referent of the noun in a given taxonomic scheme is. Animacy can have various effects on the grammar of a language, such as choice of pronoun (what/who), case endings, word order, or the form a verb takes when it is associated with that noun. In languages which demonstrate animacy, some have simple systems where nouns are either animate (e.g. people, animals) or inanimate (e.g. buildings, trees, abstract ideas), whereas others have complex hierarchical systems.

Chapter 6. REFERENCE

1. The word _____ is derived from Middle English referren, from Middle French référer, from Latin referre, 'to carry back', formed from the prefix re- and ferre, 'to bear'. A large number of words derive from this root, including referee, _____, referendum, all retaining the basic meaning of the original Latin as 'a point, place or source of origin' in terms of which something of comparable nature can be defined. A referee is the provider of this source of origin, and a referent is the possessor of the source of origin, whether it is knowledge, matter or energy.

   a. Referential density
   b. Referring expression
   c. Reference
   d. Retronym

2. A _____ is a language which, instead of acoustically conveyed sound patterns, uses visually transmitted sign patterns (manual communication, body language) to convey meaning--simultaneously combining hand shapes, orientation and movement of the hands, arms or body, and facial expressions to fluidly express a speaker's thoughts.

   Wherever communities of deaf people exist, _____s develop. Their complex spatial grammars are markedly different from the grammars of spoken languages.

   a. Sign language
   b. Speech repetition
   c. Sublanguage
   d. Transitional bilingualism

3. _____ is a notion used in the language sciences (linguistics, sociolinguistics, systemic functional linguistics, discourse analysis, pragmatics, semiotics, etc). in two different ways, namely as•verbal _____•social _____

   Verbal _____

   Verbal _____ refers to surrounding text or talk of an expression (word, sentence, conversational turn, speech act, etc).. The idea is that verbal _____ influences the way we understand the expression.

   a. Cataphora
   b. Communicative rationality
   c. Cooperative principle
   d. Context

4. . _____ is an impairment of language ability. This class of language disorder ranges from having difficulty remembering words to being completely unable to speak, read, or write.

   _____ disorders usually develop quickly as a result of head injury or stroke, but can develop slowly from a brain tumor, infection, or dementia, or can be a learning disability such as dysnomia.

   a. Aphasia
   b. Aphasia
   c. Conversational model

Chapter 6. REFERENCE

5. A _____ is a passage that explains the meaning of a term (a word, phrase or other set of symbols), or a type of thing. The term to be defined is the definiendum. A term may have many different senses or meanings.

   a. Demonym
   b. Descriptive interpretation
   c. Descriptive knowledge
   d. Definition

ANSWER KEY
Chapter 6. REFERENCE

1. c
2. a
3. d
4. b
5. d

You can take the complete Chapter Practice Test

for Chapter 6. REFERENCE
on all key terms, persons, places, and concepts.

Online 99 Cents

http://www.epub4140.6.20427.6.cram101.com/

Use www.Cram101.com for all your study needs

including Cram101's online interactive problem solving labs in

chemistry, statistics, mathematics, and more.

	Definition
	Cohort model
	Sign
	Sign language
	Reference
	Aphasia
	Implicature
	Language change
	Dialogue
	Discourse
	Metonymy
	Underspecification
	Speech perception

Chapter 7. NON-LITERAL LANGUAGE PROCESSING

CHAPTER HIGHLIGHTS & NOTES: KEY TERMS, PEOPLE, PLACES, CONCEPTS

Definition	A definition is a passage that explains the meaning of a term (a word, phrase or other set of symbols), or a type of thing. The term to be defined is the definiendum. A term may have many different senses or meanings.
Cohort model	The cohort model in psycholinguistics and neurolinguistics is a model of lexical retrieval first proposed by William Marslen-Wilson in the late 1980s. It attempts to describe how visual or auditory input (i.e., hearing or reading a word) is mapped onto a word in a hearer's lexicon. According to the model, when a person hears speech segments real-time, each speech segment 'activates' every word in the lexicon that begins with that segment, and as more segments are added, more words are ruled out, until only one word is left that still matches the input.
Sign	A sign is something that implies a connection between itself and its object. A natural sign bears a causal relation to its object--for instance, thunder is a sign of storm. A conventional sign signifies by agreement, as a full stop signifies the end of a sentence.
Sign language	A sign language is a language which, instead of acoustically conveyed sound patterns, uses visually transmitted sign patterns (manual communication, body language) to convey meaning-- simultaneously combining hand shapes, orientation and movement of the hands, arms or body, and facial expressions to fluidly express a speaker's thoughts. Wherever communities of deaf people exist, sign languages develop. Their complex spatial grammars are markedly different from the grammars of spoken languages.
Reference	The word reference is derived from Middle English referren, from Middle French référer, from Latin referre, 'to carry back', formed from the prefix re- and ferre, 'to bear'. A large number of words derive from this root, including referee, reference, referendum, all retaining the basic meaning of the original Latin as 'a point, place or source of origin' in terms of which something of comparable nature can be defined. A referee is the provider of this source of origin, and a referent is the possessor of the source of origin, whether it is knowledge, matter or energy.
Aphasia	Aphasia is an impairment of language ability. This class of language disorder ranges from having difficulty remembering words to being completely unable to speak, read, or write. Aphasia disorders usually develop quickly as a result of head injury or stroke, but can develop slowly from a brain tumor, infection, or dementia, or can be a learning disability such as dysnomia.
Implicature	Implicature is a technical term in the pragmatics subfield of linguistics, coined by H. P. Grice, which refers to what is suggested in an utterance, even though neither expressed nor strictly implied (that is, entailed) by the utterance.

Visit Cram101.com for full Practice Exams

For example, the sentence 'Mary had a baby and got married' strongly suggests that Mary had the baby before the wedding, but the sentence would still be strictly true if Mary had her baby after she got married. Further, if we add the qualification '-- not necessarily in that order' to the original sentence, then the implicature is cancelled even though the meaning of the original sentence is not altered.

Language change	Language change is the phenomenon whereby phonetic, morphological, semantic, syntactic, and other features of language vary over time. The effect on language over time is known as diachronic change. Two linguistic disciplines in particular concern themselves with studying language change: historical linguistics and sociolinguistics.
Dialogue	Dialogue is a literary and theatrical form consisting of a written or spoken conversational exchange between two or more people.
	Its chief historical origins as narrative, philosophical or didactic device are to be found in classical Greek and Indian literature, in particular in the ancient art of rhetoric.
	Having lost touch almost entirely in the 19th century with its underpinnings in rhetoric, the notion of dialogue emerged transformed in the work of cultural critics such as Mikhail Bakhtin and Paulo Freire, theologians such as Martin Buber, as an existential palliative to counter atomization and social alienation in mass industrial society.
Discourse	Discourse generally refers to 'written or spoken communication'. The following are three more specific definitions:•In semantics and discourse analysis: A generalization of the concept of conversation to all modalities and contexts.•'The totality of codified linguistic usages attached to a given type of social practice. (E.g.: legal discourse, medical discourse, religious discourse).' •In the work of Michel Foucault, and social theorists inspired by him: 'an entity of sequences of signs in that they are enouncements (enoncés).' An enouncement (l'énoncé - often translated as 'statement') is not a unity of signs, but an abstract matter that enables signs to assign specific repeatable relations to objects, subjects and other enouncements.
Metonymy	Metonymy is a figure of speech used in rhetoric in which a thing or concept is not called by its own name, but by the name of something intimately associated with that thing or concept. For instance, 'Hollywood' is used as a metonym (an instance of metonymy) for US cinema, because of the fame and cultural identity of Hollywood, a district of Los Angeles, California as the historical center of movie studios and movie stars. Another example is 'Westminster,' which is used as a metonym for the Parliament of the United Kingdom, because it is located there.
Underspecification	In theoretical linguistics, underspecification is a phenomenon in which certain features are omitted in underlying representations. Restricted underspecification theory holds that features should only be underspecified if their values are predictable.

Chapter 7. NON-LITERAL LANGUAGE PROCESSING

Speech perception	Speech perception is the process by which the sounds of language are heard, interpreted and understood. The study of speech perception is closely linked to the fields of phonetics and phonology in linguistics and cognitive psychology and perception in psychology. Research in speech perception seeks to understand how human listeners recognize speech sounds and use this information to understand spoken language.

1. _____ is an impairment of language ability. This class of language disorder ranges from having difficulty remembering words to being completely unable to speak, read, or write.

    _____ disorders usually develop quickly as a result of head injury or stroke, but can develop slowly from a brain tumor, infection, or dementia, or can be a learning disability such as dysnomia.

    a. Aphasia
    b. Aphasia
    c. Representation term
    d. Retronym

2. _____ is a technical term in the pragmatics subfield of linguistics, coined by H. P. Grice, which refers to what is suggested in an utterance, even though neither expressed nor strictly implied (that is, entailed) by the utterance. For example, the sentence 'Mary had a baby and got married' strongly suggests that Mary had the baby before the wedding, but the sentence would still be strictly true if Mary had her baby after she got married. Further, if we add the qualification '-- not necessarily in that order' to the original sentence, then the _____ is cancelled even though the meaning of the original sentence is not altered.

    a. Origo
    b. Ostensive definition
    c. Implicature
    d. Retronym

3. A _____ is a passage that explains the meaning of a term (a word, phrase or other set of symbols), or a type of thing. The term to be defined is the definiendum. A term may have many different senses or meanings.

    a. Demonym
    b. Descriptive interpretation
    c. Descriptive knowledge
    d. Definition

4. A _____ is a language which, instead of acoustically conveyed sound patterns, uses visually transmitted sign patterns (manual communication, body language) to convey meaning--simultaneously combining hand shapes, orientation and movement of the hands, arms or body, and facial expressions to fluidly express a speaker's thoughts.

    Wherever communities of deaf people exist, _____s develop. Their complex spatial grammars are markedly different from the grammars of spoken languages.

    a. Speech production
    b. Speech repetition
    c. Sign language
    d. Transitional bilingualism

5. The _____ in psycholinguistics and neurolinguistics is a model of lexical retrieval first proposed by William Marslen-Wilson in the late 1980s. It attempts to describe how visual or auditory input (i.e., hearing or reading a word) is mapped onto a word in a hearer's lexicon. According to the model, when a person hears speech segments real-time, each speech segment 'activates' every word in the lexicon that begins with that segment, and as more segments are added, more words are ruled out, until only one word is left that still matches the input.

    a. Collaborative model
    b. Competition model
    c. Conversational model
    d. Cohort model

1. b
2. c
3. d
4. c
5. d

You can take the complete Chapter Practice Test

for Chapter 7. NON-LITERAL LANGUAGE PROCESSING
on all key terms, persons, places, and concepts.

Online 99 Cents

http://www.epub4140.6.20427.7.cram101.com/

Use www.Cram101.com for all your study needs

including Cram101's online interactive problem solving labs in

chemistry, statistics, mathematics, and more.

Chapter 8. DIALOGUE

Cohort model

Dialogue

Discourse

Sign

Sign language

Reference

Audience design

Error analysis

Syntactic ambiguity

CHAPTER HIGHLIGHTS & NOTES: KEY TERMS, PEOPLE, PLACES, CONCEPTS

Cohort model	The cohort model in psycholinguistics and neurolinguistics is a model of lexical retrieval first proposed by William Marslen-Wilson in the late 1980s. It attempts to describe how visual or auditory input (i.e., hearing or reading a word) is mapped onto a word in a hearer's lexicon. According to the model, when a person hears speech segments real-time, each speech segment 'activates' every word in the lexicon that begins with that segment, and as more segments are added, more words are ruled out, until only one word is left that still matches the input.
Dialogue	Dialogue is a literary and theatrical form consisting of a written or spoken conversational exchange between two or more people. Its chief historical origins as narrative, philosophical or didactic device are to be found in classical Greek and Indian literature, in particular in the ancient art of rhetoric.

Discourse	Discourse generally refers to 'written or spoken communication'. The following are three more specific definitions:•In semantics and discourse analysis: A generalization of the concept of conversation to all modalities and contexts.•'The totality of codified linguistic usages attached to a given type of social practice. (E.g.: legal discourse, medical discourse, religious discourse).' •In the work of Michel Foucault, and social theorists inspired by him: 'an entity of sequences of signs in that they are enouncements (enoncés).' An enouncement (l'énoncé - often translated as 'statement') is not a unity of signs, but an abstract matter that enables signs to assign specific repeatable relations to objects, subjects and other enouncements.
Sign	A sign is something that implies a connection between itself and its object. A natural sign bears a causal relation to its object--for instance, thunder is a sign of storm. A conventional sign signifies by agreement, as a full stop signifies the end of a sentence.
Sign language	A sign language is a language which, instead of acoustically conveyed sound patterns, uses visually transmitted sign patterns (manual communication, body language) to convey meaning-- simultaneously combining hand shapes, orientation and movement of the hands, arms or body, and facial expressions to fluidly express a speaker's thoughts. Wherever communities of deaf people exist, sign languages develop. Their complex spatial grammars are markedly different from the grammars of spoken languages.
Reference	The word reference is derived from Middle English referren, from Middle French référer, from Latin referre, 'to carry back', formed from the prefix re- and ferre, 'to bear'. A large number of words derive from this root, including referee, reference, referendum, all retaining the basic meaning of the original Latin as 'a point, place or source of origin' in terms of which something of comparable nature can be defined. A referee is the provider of this source of origin, and a referent is the possessor of the source of origin, whether it is knowledge, matter or energy.
Audience design	Audience design is a sociolinguistic model outlined by Allan Bell in 1984 which proposes that linguistic style-shifting occurs primarily in response to a speaker's audience. According to this model, speakers adjust their speech primarily towards that of their audience in order to express solidarity or intimacy with them, or away from their audience's speech to express distance. Earlier sociolinguistic research was primarily influenced by William Labov, who studied style-shifting as a function of attention paid to speech, and who developed techniques for eliciting various styles of speech during research interviews.
Error analysis	In second language acquisition, error analysis studies the types and causes of language errors. Errors are classified according to:•modality (i.e., level of proficiency in speaking, writing, reading, listening)•linguistic levels •form (e.g., omission, insertion, substitution)•type (systematic errors/errors in competence vs.

Chapter 8. DIALOGUE

occasional errors/errors in performance)•cause (e.g., interference, interlanguage)•norm vs. system

Methodology

Error analysis in SLA was established in the 1960s by Stephen Pit Corder and colleagues. Error analysis was an alternative to contrastive analysis, an approach influenced by behaviorism through which applied linguists sought to use the formal distinctions between the learners' first and second languages to predict errors.

Syntactic ambiguity | Syntactic ambiguity is a property of sentences which may be reasonably interpreted in more than one way, or reasonably interpreted to mean more than one thing. Ambiguity may or may not involve one word having two parts of speech or homonyms.

Syntactic ambiguity arises not from the range of meanings of single words, but from the relationship between the words and clauses of a sentence, and the sentence structure implied thereby.

1. The _____ in psycholinguistics and neurolinguistics is a model of lexical retrieval first proposed by William Marslen-Wilson in the late 1980s. It attempts to describe how visual or auditory input (i.e., hearing or reading a word) is mapped onto a word in a hearer's lexicon. According to the model, when a person hears speech segments real-time, each speech segment 'activates' every word in the lexicon that begins with that segment, and as more segments are added, more words are ruled out, until only one word is left that still matches the input.

    a. Collaborative model
    b. Competition model
    c. Conversational model
    d. Cohort model

2. . _____ is a literary and theatrical form consisting of a written or spoken conversational exchange between two or more people.

    Its chief historical origins as narrative, philosophical or didactic device are to be found in classical Greek and Indian literature, in particular in the ancient art of rhetoric.

    Having lost touch almost entirely in the 19th century with its underpinnings in rhetoric, the notion of _____ emerged transformed in the work of cultural critics such as Mikhail Bakhtin and Paulo Freire, theologians such as Martin Buber, as an existential palliative to counter atomization and social alienation in mass industrial society.

    a. Dilemma

Chapter 8. DIALOGUE

   b. Dispositio

   c. Dialogue

   d. Fallacy

3. _____ generally refers to 'written or spoken communication'. The following are three more specific definitions:•In semantics and _____ analysis: A generalization of the concept of conversation to all modalities and contexts.•'The totality of codified linguistic usages attached to a given type of social practice. (E.g.: legal _____, medical _____, religious _____).' •In the work of Michel Foucault, and social theorists inspired by him: 'an entity of sequences of signs in that they are enouncements (enoncés).' An enouncement (l'énoncé - often translated as 'statement') is not a unity of signs, but an abstract matter that enables signs to assign specific repeatable relations to objects, subjects and other enouncements.

   a. Double entendre

   b. Discourse

   c. Dysphemism

   d. The Establishment

4. A _____ is something that implies a connection between itself and its object. A natural _____ bears a causal relation to its object--for instance, thunder is a _____ of storm. A conventional _____ signifies by agreement, as a full stop signifies the end of a sentence.

   a. Sign relation

   b. Sign

   c. Sign system

   d. Symbol theory

5. A _____ is a language which, instead of acoustically conveyed sound patterns, uses visually transmitted sign patterns (manual communication, body language) to convey meaning--simultaneously combining hand shapes, orientation and movement of the hands, arms or body, and facial expressions to fluidly express a speaker's thoughts.

Wherever communities of deaf people exist, _____s develop. Their complex spatial grammars are markedly different from the grammars of spoken languages.

   a. Sign language

   b. Speech repetition

   c. Sublanguage

   d. Transitional bilingualism

1. d
2. c
3. b
4. b
5. a

You can take the complete Chapter Practice Test

for Chapter 8. DIALOGUE
on all key terms, persons, places, and concepts.

Online 99 Cents

http://www.epub4140.6.20427.8.cram101.com/

Use www.Cram101.com for all your study needs

including Cram101's online interactive problem solving labs in

chemistry, statistics, mathematics, and more.

Chapter 9. LANGUAGE DEVELOPMENT IN INFANCY AND EARLY CHILDHOC

CHAPTER OUTLINE: KEY TERMS, PEOPLE, PLACES, CONCEPTS

_____ Language development

_____ Cohort model

_____ Speech perception

_____ Grammars

_____ Phoneme

_____ Linguistics

_____ Prototype theory

_____ Definition

_____ Phonotactics

_____ Syllable

_____ Error analysis

_____ Syntax

_____ Mean length of utterance

_____ Utterance

_____ Language acquisition

Language development	Language development is a process starting early in human life, when a person begins to acquire language by learning it as it is spoken and by mimicry. Children's language development moves from simple to complex. Infants start without language.
Cohort model	The cohort model in psycholinguistics and neurolinguistics is a model of lexical retrieval first proposed by William Marslen-Wilson in the late 1980s. It attempts to describe how visual or auditory input (i.e., hearing or reading a word) is mapped onto a word in a hearer's lexicon. According to the model, when a person hears speech segments real-time, each speech segment 'activates' every word in the lexicon that begins with that segment, and as more segments are added, more words are ruled out, until only one word is left that still matches the input.
Speech perception	Speech perception is the process by which the sounds of language are heard, interpreted and understood. The study of speech perception is closely linked to the fields of phonetics and phonology in linguistics and cognitive psychology and perception in psychology. Research in speech perception seeks to understand how human listeners recognize speech sounds and use this information to understand spoken language.
Grammars	Grammars: A Journal of Mathematical Research on Formal and Natural Languages is an academic journal devoted to the mathematical linguistics of formal and natural languages, published by Springer-Verlag.
Phoneme	In a language or dialect, a phoneme is the smallest segmental unit of sound employed to form meaningful contrasts between utterances. Thus a phoneme is a sound or a group of different sounds perceived to have the same function by speakers of the language or dialect in question. An example is the English phoneme /k/ (phonemes are placed between slashes in transcription), which occurs in words such as cat, kit, school, skill.
Linguistics	Linguistics is the scientific study of human language. Linguistics can be broadly broken into three categories or subfields of study: language form, language meaning, and language in context. The first is the study of language structure, or grammar.
Prototype theory	Prototype theory is a mode of graded categorization in cognitive science, where some members of a category are more central than others. For example, when asked to give an example of the concept furniture, chair is more frequently cited than, say, stool. Prototype theory has also been applied in linguistics, as part of the mapping from phonological structure to semantics.

Chapter 9. LANGUAGE DEVELOPMENT IN INFANCY AND EARLY CHILDHOOD

Definition	A definition is a passage that explains the meaning of a term (a word, phrase or other set of symbols), or a type of thing. The term to be defined is the definiendum. A term may have many different senses or meanings.
Phonotactics	Phonotactics is a branch of phonology that deals with restrictions in a language on the permissible combinations of phonemes. Phonotactics defines permissible syllable structure, consonant clusters, and vowel sequences by means of phonotactical constraints. Phonotactic constraints are language specific.
Syllable	A syllable is a unit of organization for a sequence of speech sounds. For example, the word water is composed of two syllables: wa and ter. A syllable is typically made up of a syllable nucleus (most often a vowel) with optional initial and final margins (typically, consonants).
Error analysis	In second language acquisition, error analysis studies the types and causes of language errors. Errors are classified according to:•modality (i.e., level of proficiency in speaking, writing, reading, listening)•linguistic levels •form (e.g., omission, insertion, substitution)•type (systematic errors/errors in competence vs. occasional errors/errors in performance)•cause (e.g., interference, interlanguage)•norm vs. system Methodology Error analysis in SLA was established in the 1960s by Stephen Pit Corder and colleagues. Error analysis was an alternative to contrastive analysis, an approach influenced by behaviorism through which applied linguists sought to use the formal distinctions between the learners' first and second languages to predict errors.
Syntax	In linguistics, syntax is the study of the principles and rules for constructing phrases and sentences in natural languages. In addition to referring to the overarching discipline, the term syntax is also used to refer directly to the rules and principles that govern the sentence structure of any individual language, as in 'the syntax of Modern Irish.' Modern research in syntax attempts to describe languages in terms of such rules. Many professionals in this discipline attempt to find general rules that apply to all natural languages.
Mean length of utterance	Mean Length of Utterance is a measure of linguistic productivity in children. It is traditionally calculated by collecting 100 utterances spoken by a child and dividing the number of morphemes by the number of utterances. A higher MLU is taken to indicate a higher level of language proficiency.

Utterance	In spoken language analysis an utterance is a complete unit of speech. It is generally but not always bounded by silence. It can be represented and delineated in written language in many ways.
Language acquisition	Language acquisition is the process by which humans acquire the capacity to perceive and comprehend language, as well as to produce and use words to communicate. The capacity to successfully use language requires one to pick up a range of tools including syntax, phonetics, and an extensive vocabulary. This language might be vocalized as with speech or manual as in sign.

1. _____ is the process by which humans acquire the capacity to perceive and comprehend language, as well as to produce and use words to communicate. The capacity to successfully use language requires one to pick up a range of tools including syntax, phonetics, and an extensive vocabulary. This language might be vocalized as with speech or manual as in sign.

   a. Language acquisition
   b. Language documentation
   c. Language Grid
   d. Language Log

2. In linguistics, _____ is the study of the principles and rules for constructing phrases and sentences in natural languages.

   In addition to referring to the overarching discipline, the term _____ is also used to refer directly to the rules and principles that govern the sentence structure of any individual language, as in 'the _____ of Modern Irish.' Modern research in _____ attempts to describe languages in terms of such rules. Many professionals in this discipline attempt to find general rules that apply to all natural languages.

   a. Clitic
   b. Code-mixing
   c. Syntax
   d. Consonant mutation

3. . _____ is the scientific study of human language. _____ can be broadly broken into three categories or subfields of study: language form, language meaning, and language in context.

   The first is the study of language structure, or grammar.

   a. West Coast Conference on Formal Linguistics
   b. Phonological change

Chapter 9. LANGUAGE DEVELOPMENT IN INFANCY AND EARLY CHILDHOOD

c. Linguistics

d. Phonological opacity

4. _____ is a branch of phonology that deals with restrictions in a language on the permissible combinations of phonemes. _____ defines permissible syllable structure, consonant clusters, and vowel sequences by means of phonotactical constraints.

Phonotactic constraints are language specific.

a. West Coast Conference on Formal Linguistics

b. Descriptive interpretation

c. Descriptive knowledge

d. Phonotactics

5. The _____ in psycholinguistics and neurolinguistics is a model of lexical retrieval first proposed by William Marslen-Wilson in the late 1980s. It attempts to describe how visual or auditory input (i.e., hearing or reading a word) is mapped onto a word in a hearer's lexicon. According to the model, when a person hears speech segments real-time, each speech segment 'activates' every word in the lexicon that begins with that segment, and as more segments are added, more words are ruled out, until only one word is left that still matches the input.

a. Collaborative model

b. Competition model

c. Cohort model

d. Crosslinguistic influence

1. a
2. c
3. c
4. d
5. c

You can take the complete Chapter Practice Test

for Chapter 9. LANGUAGE DEVELOPMENT IN INFANCY AND EARLY CHILDHOOD
on all key terms, persons, places, and concepts.

Online 99 Cents

http://www.epub4140.6.20427.9.cram101.com/

Use www.Cram101.com for all your study needs

including Cram101's online interactive problem solving labs in

chemistry, statistics, mathematics, and more.

CHAPTER OUTLINE: KEY TERMS, PEOPLE, PLACES, CONCEPTS

	Definition
	Speech perception
	Semantic analysis
	Lateral masking
	Formant
	Cohort model
	Homograph
	Homophone
	Phonemic awareness
	Dyslexia
	Syllable

Chapter 10. READING

CHAPTER HIGHLIGHTS & NOTES: KEY TERMS, PEOPLE, PLACES, CONCEPTS

Definition	A definition is a passage that explains the meaning of a term (a word, phrase or other set of symbols), or a type of thing. The term to be defined is the definiendum. A term may have many different senses or meanings.
Speech perception	Speech perception is the process by which the sounds of language are heard, interpreted and understood. The study of speech perception is closely linked to the fields of phonetics and phonology in linguistics and cognitive psychology and perception in psychology. Research in speech perception seeks to understand how human listeners recognize speech sounds and use this information to understand spoken language.
Semantic analysis	Semantic Analysis is a composite of the 'Semantic Analysis' and the 'Computational' components.'Semantic Analysis' refers to a formal analysis of meaning, and 'computational' refer to approaches that in principle support effective implementation..
Lateral masking	Lateral masking is a problem for the human visual perception of identical or similar entities in close proximity. This can be illustrated by the difficulty of counting the vertical bars of a barcode. In linguistics lateral masking refers to the interference a letter has on its neighbor.
Formant	Formants are defined by Gunnar Fant as 'the spectral peaks of the sound spectrum P(f)' of the voice. In speech science and phonetics, formant is also used to mean an acoustic resonance of the human vocal tract. It is often measured as an amplitude peak in the frequency spectrum of the sound, using a spectrogram (in the figure) or a spectrum analyzer, though in vowels spoken with a high fundamental frequency, as in a female or child voice, the frequency of the resonance may lie between the widely-spread harmonics and hence no peak is visible.
Cohort model	The cohort model in psycholinguistics and neurolinguistics is a model of lexical retrieval first proposed by William Marslen-Wilson in the late 1980s. It attempts to describe how visual or auditory input (i.e., hearing or reading a word) is mapped onto a word in a hearer's lexicon. According to the model, when a person hears speech segments real-time, each speech segment 'activates' every word in the lexicon that begins with that segment, and as more segments are added, more words are ruled out, until only one word is left that still matches the input.
Homograph	A homograph is a word or a group of words that share the same written form but have different meanings. When spoken, the meanings may be distinguished by different pronunciations, in which case the words are also heteronyms. Words with the same writing and pronunciation (i.e. homographs and homophones) are considered homonyms.
Homophone	A homophone is a word that is the same as another word but differs in meaning.

The words may be spelled the same, such as rose (flower) and rose (past tense of 'rise'), or differently, such as carat, caret, and carrot, or to, two, and too. Homophones that are spelled the same are also both homographs and homonyms.

Phonemic awareness

Phonemic awareness is a subset of phonological awareness in which listeners are able to hear, identify and manipulate phonemes, the smallest units of sound that can differentiate meaning. Separating the spoken word 'cat' into three distinct phonemes, /k/, /æ/, and /t/, requires phonemic awareness.

The National Reading Panel has found that phonemic awareness improves children's word reading and reading comprehension, as well as helping children learn to spell.

Dyslexia

Dyslexia is a very broad term defining a learning disability that impairs a person's fluency or comprehension accuracy in being able to read, and which can manifest itself as a difficulty with phonological awareness, phonological decoding, orthographic coding, auditory short-term memory, or rapid naming. Dyslexia is separate and distinct from reading difficulties resulting from other causes, such as a non-neurological deficiency with vision or hearing, or from poor or inadequate reading instruction. It is believed that dyslexia can affect between 5 and 10 percent of a given population although there have been no studies to indicate an accurate percentage.

Syllable

A syllable is a unit of organization for a sequence of speech sounds. For example, the word water is composed of two syllables: wa and ter. A syllable is typically made up of a syllable nucleus (most often a vowel) with optional initial and final margins (typically, consonants).

Chapter 10. READING

1. A _____ is a passage that explains the meaning of a term (a word, phrase or other set of symbols), or a type of thing. The term to be defined is the definiendum. A term may have many different senses or meanings.

    a. Definition
    b. Descriptive interpretation
    c. Descriptive knowledge
    d. Discourse

2. _____s are defined by Gunnar Fant as 'the spectral peaks of the sound spectrum P(f)' of the voice. In speech science and phonetics, _____ is also used to mean an acoustic resonance of the human vocal tract. It is often measured as an amplitude peak in the frequency spectrum of the sound, using a spectrogram (in the figure) or a spectrum analyzer, though in vowels spoken with a high fundamental frequency, as in a female or child voice, the frequency of the resonance may lie between the widely-spread harmonics and hence no peak is visible.

    a. Gay lisp
    b. Head voice
    c. Formant
    d. Laryngology

3. _____ is a composite of the '_____' and the 'Computational' components.'_____' refers to a formal analysis of meaning, and 'computational' refer to approaches that in principle support effective implementation..

    a. Computational semantics
    b. Cognitive linguistics
    c. Cognitive semantics
    d. Semantic analysis

4. _____ is the process by which the sounds of language are heard, interpreted and understood. The study of _____ is closely linked to the fields of phonetics and phonology in linguistics and cognitive psychology and perception in psychology. Research in _____ seeks to understand how human listeners recognize speech sounds and use this information to understand spoken language.

    a. Speech production
    b. Speech repetition
    c. Speech shadowing
    d. Speech perception

5. . The _____ in psycholinguistics and neurolinguistics is a model of lexical retrieval first proposed by William Marslen-Wilson in the late 1980s. It attempts to describe how visual or auditory input (i.e., hearing or reading a word) is mapped onto a word in a hearer's lexicon. According to the model, when a person hears speech segments real-time, each speech segment 'activates' every word in the lexicon that begins with that segment, and as more segments are added, more words are ruled out, until only one word is left that still matches the input.

    a. Collaborative model
    b. Cohort model

c. Conversational model
d. Crosslinguistic influence

1. a
2. c
3. d
4. d
5. b

You can take the complete Chapter Practice Test

for Chapter 10. READING
on all key terms, persons, places, and concepts.

Online 99 Cents

http://www.epub4140.6.20427.10.cram101.com/

Use www.Cram101.com for all your study needs

including Cram101's online interactive problem solving labs in

chemistry, statistics, mathematics, and more.

Chapter 11. BILINGUAL LANGUAGE PROCESSING

CHAPTER OUTLINE: KEY TERMS, PEOPLE, PLACES, CONCEPTS

	Definition
	Language processing
	Translation
	Cohort model
	False friend
	Homograph
	Sentence processing
	Syntax
	Sign
	Sign language
	Second language

CHAPTER HIGHLIGHTS & NOTES: KEY TERMS, PEOPLE, PLACES, CONCEPTS

Definition	A definition is a passage that explains the meaning of a term (a word, phrase or other set of symbols), or a type of thing. The term to be defined is the definiendum. A term may have many different senses or meanings.
Language processing	Language processing refers to the way human beings use words to communicate ideas and feelings, and how such communications are processed and understood. Thus it is how the brain creates and understands language. Most recent theories consider that this process is carried out entirely by and inside the brain.

Chapter 11. BILINGUAL LANGUAGE PROCESSING

Translation	Translation is the communication of the meaning of a source-language text by means of an equivalent target-language text. Whereas interpreting undoubtedly antedates writing, translation began only after the appearance of written literature; there exist partial translations of the Sumerian Epic of Gilgamesh (ca. 2000 BCE) into Southwest Asian languages of the second millennium BCE.
	Translators always risk inappropriate spill-over of source-language idiom and usage into the target-language translation. On the other hand, spill-overs have imported useful source-language calques and loanwords that have enriched the target languages.
Cohort model	The cohort model in psycholinguistics and neurolinguistics is a model of lexical retrieval first proposed by William Marslen-Wilson in the late 1980s. It attempts to describe how visual or auditory input (i.e., hearing or reading a word) is mapped onto a word in a hearer's lexicon. According to the model, when a person hears speech segments real-time, each speech segment 'activates' every word in the lexicon that begins with that segment, and as more segments are added, more words are ruled out, until only one word is left that still matches the input.
False friend	False friends are pairs of words or phrases in two languages or dialects (or letters in two alphabets) that look or sound similar, but differ in meaning. An example is Portuguese raro 'rare' vs. Spanish raro 'strange' .
	Often there is a partial overlap in meanings, which creates additional complications: e.g. Spanish lima, meaning 'lime' (the fruit) and 'lime' (the calcium-based material), but also 'file' (the tool).
Homograph	A homograph is a word or a group of words that share the same written form but have different meanings. When spoken, the meanings may be distinguished by different pronunciations, in which case the words are also heteronyms. Words with the same writing and pronunciation (i.e. homographs and homophones) are considered homonyms.
Sentence processing	Sentence processing takes place whenever a reader or listener processes a language utterance, either in isolation or in the context of a conversation or a text.
	Many studies of the human language comprehension process have focused on reading of single utterances (sentences) without context. Extensive research has shown, however, that language comprehension is affected also by context preceding a given utterance, as well as many other factors.
Syntax	In linguistics, syntax is the study of the principles and rules for constructing phrases and sentences in natural languages.

	In addition to referring to the overarching discipline, the term syntax is also used to refer directly to the rules and principles that govern the sentence structure of any individual language, as in 'the syntax of Modern Irish.' Modern research in syntax attempts to describe languages in terms of such rules. Many professionals in this discipline attempt to find general rules that apply to all natural languages.
Sign	A sign is something that implies a connection between itself and its object. A natural sign bears a causal relation to its object--for instance, thunder is a sign of storm. A conventional sign signifies by agreement, as a full stop signifies the end of a sentence.
Sign language	A sign language is a language which, instead of acoustically conveyed sound patterns, uses visually transmitted sign patterns (manual communication, body language) to convey meaning-- simultaneously combining hand shapes, orientation and movement of the hands, arms or body, and facial expressions to fluidly express a speaker's thoughts. Wherever communities of deaf people exist, sign languages develop. Their complex spatial grammars are markedly different from the grammars of spoken languages.
Second language	A second language is any language learned after the first language or mother tongue. Some languages, often called auxiliary languages, are used primarily as second languages or lingua francas (such as Esperanto). A person's first language may not be their dominant language, the one they use most or are most comfortable with.

Chapter 11. BILINGUAL LANGUAGE PROCESSING

1. A _____ is a language which, instead of acoustically conveyed sound patterns, uses visually transmitted sign patterns (manual communication, body language) to convey meaning--simultaneously combining hand shapes, orientation and movement of the hands, arms or body, and facial expressions to fluidly express a speaker's thoughts.

   Wherever communities of deaf people exist, _____s develop. Their complex spatial grammars are markedly different from the grammars of spoken languages.

   a. Speech production
   b. Speech repetition
   c. Sign language
   d. Transitional bilingualism

2. _____s are pairs of words or phrases in two languages or dialects (or letters in two alphabets) that look or sound similar, but differ in meaning. An example is Portuguese raro 'rare' vs. Spanish raro 'strange' .

   Often there is a partial overlap in meanings, which creates additional complications: e.g. Spanish lima, meaning 'lime' (the fruit) and 'lime' (the calcium-based material), but also 'file' (the tool).

   a. Lexical similarity
   b. Linguistic typology
   c. Mamihlapinatapai
   d. False friend

3. _____ is the communication of the meaning of a source-language text by means of an equivalent target-language text. Whereas interpreting undoubtedly antedates writing, _____ began only after the appearance of written literature; there exist partial _____s of the Sumerian Epic of Gilgamesh (ca. 2000 BCE) into Southwest Asian languages of the second millennium BCE.

   Translators always risk inappropriate spill-over of source-language idiom and usage into the target-language _____. On the other hand, spill-overs have imported useful source-language calques and loanwords that have enriched the target languages.

   a. Buddhist Hybrid English
   b. Translation
   c. Contrafactum
   d. Controlled language in machine translation

4. . A _____ is any language learned after the first language or mother tongue. Some languages, often called auxiliary languages, are used primarily as _____s or lingua francas (such as Esperanto).

   A person's first language may not be their dominant language, the one they use most or are most comfortable with.

   a. Shabda
   b. Second language
   c. Sign language

5. A _____ is a passage that explains the meaning of a term (a word, phrase or other set of symbols), or a type of thing. The term to be defined is the definiendum. A term may have many different senses or meanings.

    a. Demonym
    b. Descriptive interpretation
    c. Definition
    d. Discourse

1. c
2. d
3. b
4. b
5. c

You can take the complete Chapter Practice Test

for Chapter 11. BILINGUAL LANGUAGE PROCESSING
on all key terms, persons, places, and concepts.

Online 99 Cents

http://www.epub4140.6.20427.11.cram101.com/

Use www.Cram101.com for all your study needs

including Cram101's online interactive problem solving labs in

chemistry, statistics, mathematics, and more.

CHAPTER OUTLINE: KEY TERMS, PEOPLE, PLACES, CONCEPTS

Sign

Sign language

Aphasia

Allophone

Cohort model

Language change

Language development

Sign system

Pidgin

Speech perception

Phonotactics

Semantic analysis

Language processing

Chapter 12. SIGN LANGUAGE

Sign	A sign is something that implies a connection between itself and its object. A natural sign bears a causal relation to its object--for instance, thunder is a sign of storm. A conventional sign signifies by agreement, as a full stop signifies the end of a sentence.
Sign language	A sign language is a language which, instead of acoustically conveyed sound patterns, uses visually transmitted sign patterns (manual communication, body language) to convey meaning-- simultaneously combining hand shapes, orientation and movement of the hands, arms or body, and facial expressions to fluidly express a speaker's thoughts.
	Wherever communities of deaf people exist, sign languages develop. Their complex spatial grammars are markedly different from the grammars of spoken languages.
Aphasia	Aphasia is an impairment of language ability. This class of language disorder ranges from having difficulty remembering words to being completely unable to speak, read, or write.
	Aphasia disorders usually develop quickly as a result of head injury or stroke, but can develop slowly from a brain tumor, infection, or dementia, or can be a learning disability such as dysnomia.
Allophone	In phonology, an allophone is one of a set of multiple possible spoken sounds (or phones) used to pronounce a single phoneme. For example, [p?] (as in pin) and [p] (as in spin) are allophones for the phoneme /p/ in the English language. Although a phoneme's allophones are all alternative pronunciations for a phoneme, the specific allophone selected in a given situation is often predictable.
Cohort model	The cohort model in psycholinguistics and neurolinguistics is a model of lexical retrieval first proposed by William Marslen-Wilson in the late 1980s. It attempts to describe how visual or auditory input (i.e., hearing or reading a word) is mapped onto a word in a hearer's lexicon. According to the model, when a person hears speech segments real-time, each speech segment 'activates' every word in the lexicon that begins with that segment, and as more segments are added, more words are ruled out, until only one word is left that still matches the input.
Language change	Language change is the phenomenon whereby phonetic, morphological, semantic, syntactic, and other features of language vary over time. The effect on language over time is known as diachronic change. Two linguistic disciplines in particular concern themselves with studying language change: historical linguistics and sociolinguistics.
Language development	Language development is a process starting early in human life, when a person begins to acquire language by learning it as it is spoken and by mimicry. Children's language development moves from simple to complex.

Sign system	A sign system is a key concept in semiotics and is used to refer to any system of signs and relations between signs. The term language is frequently used as a synonym for a sign-system. However, the term sign-system is preferable to the term language for a number of reasons.
Pidgin	A pidgin language, is a simplified language that develops as a means of communication between two or more groups that do not have a language in common. It is most commonly employed in situations such as trade, or where both groups speak languages different from the language of the country in which they reside (but where there is no common language between the groups). Fundamentally, a pidgin is a simplified means of linguistic communication, as it is constructed impromptu, or by convention, between individuals or groups of people.
Speech perception	Speech perception is the process by which the sounds of language are heard, interpreted and understood. The study of speech perception is closely linked to the fields of phonetics and phonology in linguistics and cognitive psychology and perception in psychology. Research in speech perception seeks to understand how human listeners recognize speech sounds and use this information to understand spoken language.
Phonotactics	Phonotactics is a branch of phonology that deals with restrictions in a language on the permissible combinations of phonemes. Phonotactics defines permissible syllable structure, consonant clusters, and vowel sequences by means of phonotactical constraints. Phonotactic constraints are language specific.
Semantic analysis	Semantic Analysis is a composite of the 'Semantic Analysis' and the 'Computational' components.'Semantic Analysis' refers to a formal analysis of meaning, and 'computational' refer to approaches that in principle support effective implementation..
Language processing	Language processing refers to the way human beings use words to communicate ideas and feelings, and how such communications are processed and understood. Thus it is how the brain creates and understands language. Most recent theories consider that this process is carried out entirely by and inside the brain.

Chapter 12. SIGN LANGUAGE

1. A _____ is something that implies a connection between itself and its object. A natural _____ bears a causal relation to its object--for instance, thunder is a _____ of storm. A conventional _____ signifies by agreement, as a full stop signifies the end of a sentence.

   a. Sign relation
   b. Sign
   c. Sign system
   d. Symbol theory

2. _____ is a branch of phonology that deals with restrictions in a language on the permissible combinations of phonemes. _____ defines permissible syllable structure, consonant clusters, and vowel sequences by means of phonotactical constraints.

   Phonotactic constraints are language specific.

   a. West Coast Conference on Formal Linguistics
   b. Speech repetition
   c. Phonotactics
   d. Spelling pronunciation

3. A _____ is a language which, instead of acoustically conveyed sound patterns, uses visually transmitted sign patterns (manual communication, body language) to convey meaning--simultaneously combining hand shapes, orientation and movement of the hands, arms or body, and facial expressions to fluidly express a speaker's thoughts.

   Wherever communities of deaf people exist, _____s develop. Their complex spatial grammars are markedly different from the grammars of spoken languages.

   a. Speech production
   b. Sign language
   c. Sublanguage
   d. Transitional bilingualism

4. _____ is an impairment of language ability. This class of language disorder ranges from having difficulty remembering words to being completely unable to speak, read, or write.

   _____ disorders usually develop quickly as a result of head injury or stroke, but can develop slowly from a brain tumor, infection, or dementia, or can be a learning disability such as dysnomia.

   a. Aphasia
   b. Speech repetition
   c. Sublanguage
   d. Transitional bilingualism

5. . In phonology, an _____ is one of a set of multiple possible spoken sounds (or phones) used to pronounce a single phoneme. For example, [p?] (as in pin) and [p] (as in spin) are _____s for the phoneme /p/ in the English language.

Chapter 12. SIGN LANGUAGE

Visit Cram101.com for full Practice Exams

Although a phoneme's _____s are all alternative pronunciations for a phoneme, the specific _____ selected in a given situation is often predictable.

a. Allophone
b. Alphaphonetic pronunciation
c. Apocope
d. Articulatory phonology

1. b
2. c
3. b
4. a
5. a

You can take the complete Chapter Practice Test

for Chapter 12. SIGN LANGUAGE
on all key terms, persons, places, and concepts.

Online 99 Cents

http://www.epub4140.6.20427.12.cram101.com/

Use www.Cram101.com for all your study needs

including Cram101's online interactive problem solving labs in

chemistry, statistics, mathematics, and more.

Chapter 13. APHASIA

CHAPTER OUTLINE: KEY TERMS, PEOPLE, PLACES, CONCEPTS

	Aphasia
	Cohort model
	Aphasiology
	Definition
	Speech perception
	Reference
	Sign
	Sign language
	Syntax
	Semantic analysis

Visit Cram101.com for full Practice Exams

Chapter 13. APHASIA

Aphasia	Aphasia is an impairment of language ability. This class of language disorder ranges from having difficulty remembering words to being completely unable to speak, read, or write. Aphasia disorders usually develop quickly as a result of head injury or stroke, but can develop slowly from a brain tumor, infection, or dementia, or can be a learning disability such as dysnomia.
Cohort model	The cohort model in psycholinguistics and neurolinguistics is a model of lexical retrieval first proposed by William Marslen-Wilson in the late 1980s. It attempts to describe how visual or auditory input (i.e., hearing or reading a word) is mapped onto a word in a hearer's lexicon. According to the model, when a person hears speech segments real-time, each speech segment 'activates' every word in the lexicon that begins with that segment, and as more segments are added, more words are ruled out, until only one word is left that still matches the input.
Aphasiology	Aphasiology is the study of linguistic problems resulting from brain damage. It is also the name of a scientific journal covering the area. These specific deficits, termed aphasias, may be defined as impairments of language production or comprehension that cannot be attributed to trivial causes such as deafness or oral paralysis.
Definition	A definition is a passage that explains the meaning of a term (a word, phrase or other set of symbols), or a type of thing. The term to be defined is the definiendum. A term may have many different senses or meanings.
Speech perception	Speech perception is the process by which the sounds of language are heard, interpreted and understood. The study of speech perception is closely linked to the fields of phonetics and phonology in linguistics and cognitive psychology and perception in psychology. Research in speech perception seeks to understand how human listeners recognize speech sounds and use this information to understand spoken language.
Reference	The word reference is derived from Middle English referren, from Middle French référer, from Latin referre, 'to carry back', formed from the prefix re- and ferre, 'to bear'. A large number of words derive from this root, including referee, reference, referendum, all retaining the basic meaning of the original Latin as 'a point, place or source of origin' in terms of which something of comparable nature can be defined. A referee is the provider of this source of origin, and a referent is the possessor of the source of origin, whether it is knowledge, matter or energy.
Sign	A sign is something that implies a connection between itself and its object. A natural sign bears a causal relation to its object--for instance, thunder is a sign of storm.

Chapter 13. APHASIA

| Sign language | A sign language is a language which, instead of acoustically conveyed sound patterns, uses visually transmitted sign patterns (manual communication, body language) to convey meaning--simultaneously combining hand shapes, orientation and movement of the hands, arms or body, and facial expressions to fluidly express a speaker's thoughts.

Wherever communities of deaf people exist, sign languages develop. Their complex spatial grammars are markedly different from the grammars of spoken languages. |
| Syntax | In linguistics, syntax is the study of the principles and rules for constructing phrases and sentences in natural languages.

In addition to referring to the overarching discipline, the term syntax is also used to refer directly to the rules and principles that govern the sentence structure of any individual language, as in 'the syntax of Modern Irish.' Modern research in syntax attempts to describe languages in terms of such rules. Many professionals in this discipline attempt to find general rules that apply to all natural languages. |
| Semantic analysis | Semantic Analysis is a composite of the 'Semantic Analysis' and the 'Computational' components.'Semantic Analysis' refers to a formal analysis of meaning, and 'computational' refer to approaches that in principle support effective implementation.. |

1. _____ is the study of linguistic problems resulting from brain damage. It is also the name of a scientific journal covering the area.

These specific deficits, termed aphasias, may be defined as impairments of language production or comprehension that cannot be attributed to trivial causes such as deafness or oral paralysis.

   a. Early left anterior negativity
   b. Competition model
   c. Conversational model
   d. Aphasiology

2. . The _____ in psycholinguistics and neurolinguistics is a model of lexical retrieval first proposed by William Marslen-Wilson in the late 1980s. It attempts to describe how visual or auditory input (i.e., hearing or reading a word) is mapped onto a word in a hearer's lexicon. According to the model, when a person hears speech segments real-time, each speech segment 'activates' every word in the lexicon that begins with that segment, and as more segments are added, more words are ruled out, until only one word is left that still matches the input.

   a. Cohort model

Chapter 13. APHASIA

Visit Cram101.com for full Practice Exams

b. Competition model

c. Conversational model

d. Crosslinguistic influence

3. _____ is the process by which the sounds of language are heard, interpreted and understood. The study of _____ is closely linked to the fields of phonetics and phonology in linguistics and cognitive psychology and perception in psychology. Research in _____ seeks to understand how human listeners recognize speech sounds and use this information to understand spoken language.

a. Speech perception

b. Speech repetition

c. Speech shadowing

d. Spelling pronunciation

4. _____ is an impairment of language ability. This class of language disorder ranges from having difficulty remembering words to being completely unable to speak, read, or write.

_____ disorders usually develop quickly as a result of head injury or stroke, but can develop slowly from a brain tumor, infection, or dementia, or can be a learning disability such as dysnomia.

a. Aphasia

b. Acephalous society

c. Aphasia

d. Actor-network theory

5. A _____ is a passage that explains the meaning of a term (a word, phrase or other set of symbols), or a type of thing. The term to be defined is the definiendum. A term may have many different senses or meanings.

a. Demonym

b. Definition

c. Descriptive knowledge

d. Discourse

ANSWER KEY
Chapter 13. APHASIA

1. d
2. a
3. a
4. c
5. b

You can take the complete Chapter Practice Test

for Chapter 13. APHASIA
on all key terms, persons, places, and concepts.

Online 99 Cents

http://www.epub4140.6.20427.13.cram101.com/

Use www.Cram101.com for all your study needs

including Cram101's online interactive problem solving labs in

chemistry, statistics, mathematics, and more.

CHAPTER OUTLINE: KEY TERMS, PEOPLE, PLACES, CONCEPTS

Cohort model

Aphasia

Language processing

Definition

Speech perception

Language identification

Dialogue

Sign

Sign language

Polysemy

Discourse

Reference

Syntax

Dyslexia

Chapter 14. RIGHT-HEMISPHERE LANGUAGE FUNCTION

Cohort model	The cohort model in psycholinguistics and neurolinguistics is a model of lexical retrieval first proposed by William Marslen-Wilson in the late 1980s. It attempts to describe how visual or auditory input (i.e., hearing or reading a word) is mapped onto a word in a hearer's lexicon. According to the model, when a person hears speech segments real-time, each speech segment 'activates' every word in the lexicon that begins with that segment, and as more segments are added, more words are ruled out, until only one word is left that still matches the input.
Aphasia	Aphasia is an impairment of language ability. This class of language disorder ranges from having difficulty remembering words to being completely unable to speak, read, or write. Aphasia disorders usually develop quickly as a result of head injury or stroke, but can develop slowly from a brain tumor, infection, or dementia, or can be a learning disability such as dysnomia.
Language processing	Language processing refers to the way human beings use words to communicate ideas and feelings, and how such communications are processed and understood. Thus it is how the brain creates and understands language. Most recent theories consider that this process is carried out entirely by and inside the brain.
Definition	A definition is a passage that explains the meaning of a term (a word, phrase or other set of symbols), or a type of thing. The term to be defined is the definiendum. A term may have many different senses or meanings.
Speech perception	Speech perception is the process by which the sounds of language are heard, interpreted and understood. The study of speech perception is closely linked to the fields of phonetics and phonology in linguistics and cognitive psychology and perception in psychology. Research in speech perception seeks to understand how human listeners recognize speech sounds and use this information to understand spoken language.
Language identification	Language identification is the process of determining which natural language given content is in. Traditionally, identification of written language - as practiced, for instance, in library science - has relied on manually identifying frequent words and letters known to be characteristic of particular languages. More recently, computational approaches have been applied to the problem, by viewing language identification as a kind of text categorization, a Natural Language Processing approach which relies on statistical methods.
Dialogue	Dialogue is a literary and theatrical form consisting of a written or spoken conversational exchange between two or more people.

	Its chief historical origins as narrative, philosophical or didactic device are to be found in classical Greek and Indian literature, in particular in the ancient art of rhetoric.

Having lost touch almost entirely in the 19th century with its underpinnings in rhetoric, the notion of dialogue emerged transformed in the work of cultural critics such as Mikhail Bakhtin and Paulo Freire, theologians such as Martin Buber, as an existential palliative to counter atomization and social alienation in mass industrial society. |
| Sign | A sign is something that implies a connection between itself and its object. A natural sign bears a causal relation to its object--for instance, thunder is a sign of storm. A conventional sign signifies by agreement, as a full stop signifies the end of a sentence. |
| Sign language | A sign language is a language which, instead of acoustically conveyed sound patterns, uses visually transmitted sign patterns (manual communication, body language) to convey meaning-- simultaneously combining hand shapes, orientation and movement of the hands, arms or body, and facial expressions to fluidly express a speaker's thoughts.

Wherever communities of deaf people exist, sign languages develop. Their complex spatial grammars are markedly different from the grammars of spoken languages. |
| Polysemy | Polysemy is the capacity for a sign (e.g., a word, phrase, etc). or signs to have multiple meanings (sememes), i.e., a large semantic field.

Charles Fillmore and Beryl Atkins' definition stipulates three elements: (i) the various senses of a polysemous word have a central origin, (ii) the links between these senses form a network, and (iii) understanding the 'inner' one contributes to understanding of the 'outer' one. |
| Discourse | Discourse generally refers to 'written or spoken communication'. The following are three more specific definitions:•In semantics and discourse analysis: A generalization of the concept of conversation to all modalities and contexts.•'The totality of codified linguistic usages attached to a given type of social practice. (E.g.: legal discourse, medical discourse, religious discourse).' •In the work of Michel Foucault, and social theorists inspired by him: 'an entity of sequences of signs in that they are enouncements (enoncés).' An enouncement (l'énoncé - often translated as 'statement') is not a unity of signs, but an abstract matter that enables signs to assign specific repeatable relations to objects, subjects and other enouncements. |
| Reference | The word reference is derived from Middle English referren, from Middle French référer, from Latin referre, 'to carry back', formed from the prefix re- and ferre, 'to bear'. |

	A large number of words derive from this root, including referee, reference, referendum, all retaining the basic meaning of the original Latin as 'a point, place or source of origin' in terms of which something of comparable nature can be defined. A referee is the provider of this source of origin, and a referent is the possessor of the source of origin, whether it is knowledge, matter or energy.
Syntax	In linguistics, syntax is the study of the principles and rules for constructing phrases and sentences in natural languages. In addition to referring to the overarching discipline, the term syntax is also used to refer directly to the rules and principles that govern the sentence structure of any individual language, as in 'the syntax of Modern Irish.' Modern research in syntax attempts to describe languages in terms of such rules. Many professionals in this discipline attempt to find general rules that apply to all natural languages.
Dyslexia	Dyslexia is a very broad term defining a learning disability that impairs a person's fluency or comprehension accuracy in being able to read, and which can manifest itself as a difficulty with phonological awareness, phonological decoding, orthographic coding, auditory short-term memory, or rapid naming. Dyslexia is separate and distinct from reading difficulties resulting from other causes, such as a non-neurological deficiency with vision or hearing, or from poor or inadequate reading instruction. It is believed that dyslexia can affect between 5 and 10 percent of a given population although there have been no studies to indicate an accurate percentage.

1. _____ is a very broad term defining a learning disability that impairs a person's fluency or comprehension accuracy in being able to read, and which can manifest itself as a difficulty with phonological awareness, phonological decoding, orthographic coding, auditory short-term memory, or rapid naming. _____ is separate and distinct from reading difficulties resulting from other causes, such as a non-neurological deficiency with vision or hearing, or from poor or inadequate reading instruction. It is believed that _____ can affect between 5 and 10 percent of a given population although there have been no studies to indicate an accurate percentage.

   a. Dyslexia
   b. Dyslexia research
   c. Genetic research into dyslexia
   d. Greengate School

2. . The _____ in psycholinguistics and neurolinguistics is a model of lexical retrieval first proposed by William Marslen-Wilson in the late 1980s. It attempts to describe how visual or auditory input (i.e., hearing or reading a word) is mapped onto a word in a hearer's lexicon. According to the model, when a person hears speech segments real-time, each speech segment 'activates' every word in the lexicon that begins with that segment, and as more segments are added, more words are ruled out, until only one word is left that still matches the input.

a. Collaborative model
b. Competition model
c. Cohort model
d. Crosslinguistic influence

3. _____ is the process by which the sounds of language are heard, interpreted and understood. The study of _____ is closely linked to the fields of phonetics and phonology in linguistics and cognitive psychology and perception in psychology. Research in _____ seeks to understand how human listeners recognize speech sounds and use this information to understand spoken language.

a. Speech production
b. Speech repetition
c. Speech shadowing
d. Speech perception

4. The word _____ is derived from Middle English referren, from Middle French référer, from Latin referre, 'to carry back', formed from the prefix re- and ferre, 'to bear'. A large number of words derive from this root, including referee, _____, referendum, all retaining the basic meaning of the original Latin as 'a point, place or source of origin' in terms of which something of comparable nature can be defined. A referee is the provider of this source of origin, and a referent is the possessor of the source of origin, whether it is knowledge, matter or energy.

a. Reference
b. Referring expression
c. Representation term
d. Retronym

5. _____ is the capacity for a sign (e.g., a word, phrase, etc). or signs to have multiple meanings (sememes), i.e., a large semantic field.

Charles Fillmore and Beryl Atkins' definition stipulates three elements: (i) the various senses of a polysemous word have a central origin, (ii) the links between these senses form a network, and (iii) understanding the 'inner' one contributes to understanding of the 'outer' one.

a. Polysemy
b. Prediction in language comprehension
c. Propositional attitude
d. Psychoanalytic conceptions of language

1. a
2. c
3. d
4. a
5. a

You can take the complete Chapter Practice Test

for Chapter 14. RIGHT-HEMISPHERE LANGUAGE FUNCTION
on all key terms, persons, places, and concepts.

Online 99 Cents

http://www.epub4140.6.20427.14.cram101.com/

Use www.Cram101.com for all your study needs

including Cram101's online interactive problem solving labs in

chemistry, statistics, mathematics, and more.

Other Cram101 e-Books and Tests

Want More?
Cram101.com...

Cram101.com provides the outlines and highlights of your
textbooks, just like this e-StudyGuide, but also gives you the
PRACTICE TESTS, and other exclusive study tools for all of your
textbooks.

Learn More. *Just click*
http://www.cram101.com/

Lightning Source UK Ltd.
Milton Keynes UK
UKHW050943080520
362982UK00003B/145